EXPOSING TORTURE

Centuries of Cruelty

HAL MARCOVITZ

TWENTY-FIRST CENTURY BOOKS / MINNEAPOLIS

Twenty-First Century Books
A division of Lerner Publishing Group, Inc.
241 First Avenue North
Minneapolis, MN 55401 USA

Main body text set in Gamma ITC Std Medium 10/15.
Typeface provided by International Typeface Corp.

For reading levels and more information, look up this title at www.lernerbooks.com.

Library of Congress Cataloging-in-Publication Data

Marcovitz, Hal.
    Exposing torture : centuries of cruelty / by Hal Marcovitz.
        pages   cm
    Includes bibliographical references and index.
    ISBN 978-1-4677-5049-3 (lib. bdg. : alk. paper)
    ISBN 978-1-4677-6306-6 (ebook)
    1. Torture—History—Juvenile literature. 2. Crimes against humanity—Juvenile literature. I. Title.
    HV8593.M334 2015
    364.6'7—dc23   2014003211

Manufactured in the United States of America
1 - VI - 12/31/14

TABLE *of* CONTENTS

Free Roza Tuletaeva!

Join the campaign!

Human rights defenders = everyday heroes

FRONT LINE DEFENDERS

TAKE ACTION NOW! Demand that Roza and the other six protestors that are still in custody be released immediately.

Additional information:

Kazakhstan country page

Roza Tuletaeva - profile and appeals issued by Front Line Defenders

December 2013 (Libcom.org) - "Roza is a leader: that's why they jailed her"

June 2012 (Jamestown Foundation) - Zhanaozen Trials: Former Oil Executive Receives the longest Prison Punishment

June 2012 (Chtodelat news) - Esenbek Ukteshbayev on the Trade Union Struggle in Kazakhstan

Front Line Defenders issued urgent appeals and news items about Roza Tuletaeva:

17 January 2014 - Human rights defender Ms Roza Tuletaeva to be transferred to settlement colony

In 2011 Roza Tuletaeva, a labor activist in Kazakhstan, was arrested, tortured, and imprisoned for organizing for workers' rights. Human rights groups want to tell her story to people around the world and to pressure the government in Kazakhstan to release her from prison. A human rights organization called Front Line Defenders created a website *(above)* to draw attention to Tuletaeva's plight.

INTRODUCTION

Pain and Suffering

In April 2012, oil field worker and labor activist Roza Tuletaeva went on trial for organizing labor demonstrations the previous year in the central Asian nation of Kazakhstan. During her trial, she testified that while in jail, interrogators had suspended her from the ceiling of her cell by her hair, brought her to near suffocation by covering her head with a plastic bag, and then sexually abused her. The interrogators also threatened to harm Tuletaeva's fourteen-year-old daughter. The torture was designed to force Tuletaeva to confess to crimes and to implicate her fellow demonstrators in illegal activities. But she did not confess, and she refused to provide evidence against the other strikers. The court found her guilty of organizing mass disorder and sentenced her to five years in prison.

Tuletaeva's experience is not unusual in Kazakhstan. The nation is ruled by dictator Nursultan Nazarbayev, who has held power since 1991 and oversees one of the most repressive regimes in the world. International human rights advocates say that Nazarbayev maintains power partly by employing torture to silence his critics. During the 2011 demonstration,

This illustration of a Chinese torture method appeared in the French periodical *Le Tour du Monde* (Tour of the World) in 1864. It shows two men powering a screw device to crush a victim between two giant slabs of stone.

the police killed fourteen demonstrators and wounded more than sixty others. Dozens of demonstrators, including Tuletaeva, were arrested. According to the human rights group Amnesty International, "Eyewitnesses claimed that the detainees were kept incommunicado in overcrowded cells, that they had been stripped naked, beaten, kicked and doused with cold water. At least one man died as a result of the torture."

In an interview posted on the human rights website libcom. org, one of Tuletaeva's oil field coworkers, who identified herself only as Tatiana M., explained that the Nazarbayev government wanted to silence Tuletaeva because she represented a threat to the regime. "Roza was . . . an informal leader [of government opposition]," Tatiana said. "People trusted her; workers followed her lead. . . . Whatever anyone thought of her, they had to listen to what she said, because she had that influence. . . . That's why they put her on trial and put her in jail." As of 2014, Tuletaeva remained in prison despite calls from international human rights groups to release her.

A LONG AND BRUTAL HISTORY

Torture has been a part of global human culture for thousands of years. The ancient Greeks practiced torture, referring to their interrogation methods as *atraktos*, which means "spindle." The ancient Romans subjected their enemies to *tortura*, a Latin word that means "twist." Both terms stem from ancient methods that involved spinning or twisting the bodies of torture victims to cause severe pain and injury and sometimes death. In ancient China, torture methods included beatings; whippings; crushing fingers; and cutting off victims' hands, feet, or noses. Throughout the centuries, interrogators have used torture to instill fear, to control unruly populations, and to extract information and confessions from victims.

Well into the modern age, armies and governments have used torture in times of war to gain intelligence from rebels and foreign prisoners. Those operating outside the law, such as mobsters and terrorists, have also used torture. Says Henry Shue, professor of politics and international relations at Oxford University in England, "No other practice except slavery is so universally condemned in law and human convention. Yet, unlike slavery, which is still most definitely practiced but affects relatively few people, torture is widespread and growing."

Amnesty International reports that in the twenty-first century, 112 governments explicitly authorize torture. Why is torture so common? And why does it persist in a century when so many world leaders and global citizens passionately support human rights? Is torture an effective means of controlling human behavior? Can it help root out information about terrorism and prevent widespread destruction and loss of human life? Or is torture an unavoidable and dark component of human psychology, inflicted to gain and maintain control by exerting pain and suffering?

Torturers of the European Inquisition used spike chairs such as this one to extract confessions from suspected heretics. The victim was strapped tightly into the chair. Spikes punctured the back, buttocks, arms, legs, hands, and feet.

CHAPTER ONE

Cruel and Unusual Punishment

Throughout human history, torturers have inflicted excruciating agony on their victims. Babylonians, Hebrews, and other ancient peoples of the Middle East practiced flogging, flaying, burning, and stoning of criminals and enemies. In ancient Egypt, public whippings were a common punishment for crimes. The number and intensity of lashings increased with the seriousness of the offense. The rape of a slave, one of the most serious offenses in ancient Egypt, could bring as many as one thousand lashes. The punishment for people who murdered their parents—often to gain their wealth—were whippings that stripped the flesh from their bodies. Torturers increased the suffering by rolling the murderer through thorny weeds, which pierced exposed muscles and tendons. If, after this ordeal, the person was still alive, he or she was tossed into an open fire to burn to death.

The ancient Greeks regarded themselves as an enlightened people, well versed in sophisticated mathematics, sciences, drama, philosophy, and athletics. Yet they too practiced torture.

In the first century CE, Roman historian Quintus Curtius Rufus wrote a biography of the Macedonian conqueror Alexander the Great. This illustration appeared in a French edition of the book, printed in the 1300s. The picture shows Alexander's soldiers torturing an enemy nobleman named Calixten Cephobe. He is strung up by his wrists. A man uses a pulley to hoist him off the ground.

To punish criminals or to extract confessions from accused criminals, the Greeks employed a wooden frame called a rack. The accused was strapped onto the rack, with all four limbs tied to mechanical devices called winches. Torturers turned the winches slowly, eventually tearing the victim's ligaments and even pulling limbs from their sockets. Just a few turns of the winch were horrifically painful and usually all it took to extract a confession.

The Greeks also tied accused criminals flat against the spokes of the wheels of carts, which were then pulled by animals over rough city streets. At the least, a ride on the wheel was a disorienting and dizzying experience. At its worst, the ride led to cerebral hemorrhage (bleeding in the brain) and heart attack. Many victims died from asphyxiation by drowning in their own vomit. The Greek philosopher Aristotle, one of the most well-respected thinkers of the ancient Western world, endorsed the wheel as a way of extracting the truth from accused criminals. He described information gleaned through torture as "a sort of evidence that appears to carry with it absolute credibility."

THE CRUELTY OF CRUCIFIXION

Anybody who has entered a Christian church or has otherwise seen an image of Jesus on the cross is familiar with crucifixion— killing someone by binding or nailing the wrists or hands to a cross. Historians believe that the ancient Hebrews were the first to use crucifixion, and ancient Romans embraced crucifixion as their preferred method of torture and execution.

After conquering lands in Spain, Greece, and North Africa, the Romans used crucifixion to control their new and often unruly subjects. In a well-known uprising in 73 BCE that has been chronicled in popular films, music, and literature, the Greek-born gladiator-slave Spartacus organized an army of about seventy thousand runaway slaves. The slave army defeated soldiers of the Roman Republic and took control of parts of central and southern Italy. After splitting into two groups, one led by Spartacus, the slaves were ultimately defeated by Roman forces in 71 BCE. Six thousand of Spartacus's followers were captured and publicly crucified on crosses along the Appian Way, a major road leading to Rome. Says historian Will Durant, "Their rotting bodies were left to hang for months, so that all masters might take comfort, and all slaves take heed."

In its time, crucifixion was the most torturous and painful form of punishment. In the most merciful form of crucifixion, the victim was bound by his hands and feet to a cross fashioned from timbers. The cross was hoisted upright and positioned for stability in a hole dug into the earth. Victims could rest their

In 1878 Russian painter Fedor Andreevich Bronnikov made this picture of crucifixion as practiced by the ancient Romans. Victims were bound or nailed by their hands to crosses and left to hang. The torturous position made breathing difficult. After a few days, victims died of suffocation, heart failure, or infection caused by the wounds in their hands.

feet on a small wooden platform underneath their legs, but the arms and shoulders bore most of the body's weight. As the arms separated from the shoulder sockets, the pain grew unbearable. Most of the pressure, though, found its way to the victim's diaphragm, making breathing difficult. It was not unusual for victims of crucifixion to linger for several days before dying of suffocation or heart failure.

In a much more brutal form of crucifixion, nails were driven through a victim's hands, pinning the person to the cross. Executioners sometimes used a sledgehammer to smash the victim's knees. The wounds from the nails became painfully infected, and with broken knees and the onset of exhaustion, the victim was generally unable to lift his body enough to breathe. He typically died a slow death from infection and asphyxiation.

EXPOSING TORTURE

PUNISHMENTS OF THE MIDDLE AGES

In the fifth century of the Common Era, Visigoths and other Germanic peoples conquered the Roman Empire and Europe entered the Middle Ages (about 500 to 1500 CE). During this brutal era of European history, vindictive and marauding warriors spared few enemies caught in their paths. In 870, for example, Viking warriors from Scandinavia conquered East Anglia, part of Britain. After capturing Edmund, the East Anglian king, the Vikings tortured the king by whipping him mercilessly. Then they chopped off his head.

The English practiced their own forms of torture. In the eleventh century, for example, King William I, known as William the Conqueror, was quick to order the torture of any followers he suspected of duplicity. The torture usually took the form of castration as well as gouging out the eyes of the victim.

One of the first descriptions of torture in European literature appears in the twelfth-century French poem *La Chanson de Roland (The Song of Roland)*, which tells of the ninth-century reign of the Frankish emperor Charlemagne. In verse, the anonymous poet describes tortures inflicted on the traitor Count Ganelon:

> *They pluck the beard from off his chin and face.*
> *With four sound thumps each gives him a good*
> *   baste* [beating],
> *With sticks . . . they pound him and they paste,*
> *And round his neck they fasten a strong chain,*
> *Right well they chain him like a bear in a cage;*
> *Now on a pack-horse they've hoisted him in shame.*

In the fourteenth century, Italian poet Dante Alighieri wrote a classic three-part poem known as *The Divine Comedy*. In the most renowned section, *Inferno*, Dante describes a fictional tour through the underworld guided by the ancient Roman poet Virgil. As Dante and Virgil descend deeper into hell, readers learn about all manner of torture that awaits sinners in the afterlife.

Some are fantastical. For instance, at the time, fortune-tellers were viewed as sinners for claiming to know what most people believed only God could know—the future. In Dante's poem, fortune-tellers are doomed to hell, where their heads are twisted around to face backward. They must always look back instead of forward into the future.

The Italian painter Sandro Botticelli made illustrations for an edition of *The Divine Comedy* published in 1481. This scene shows the tormented residents of one section of hell—an area reserved for panderers, seducers, and flatterers. Some are being whipped by demons. Others are immersed in human excrement.

EXPOSING TORTURE

Many of the tortures described by Dante were drawn from real punishments used in Europe during the Middle Ages. During this era, prisons were dark, dank, and foul smelling. Prisoners, naked or clothed in the barest of rags, were chained to cold stone walls or floors. In Dante's version of hell, sinners are kept in similar surroundings. Dante also describes the fate that awaits hypocrites in hell. He finds them clothed in heavy lead capes, which they are forced to wear forever. He writes:

> O weary mantle [cape] for eternity!
> Once more we turned to the left, and by their side
> Paced on, intent upon their mournful cry.

The lead cape punishment was no figment of Dante's imagination. He borrowed it directly from the torture chambers of Fredrick II, king of the Holy Roman Empire in central Europe, who ruled from 1220 to 1250. Frederick's enemies were forced to wear the lead garments and were then hoisted into cauldrons (large pots) of boiling water. The hot water melted the lead, which peeled the skin off the prisoners. But Dante makes the wry observation in his poem that "King Frederick's [capes] would have seemed feather-light" in comparison to those used in hell.

TORTURES OF THE INQUISITION

The period of European history known as the Inquisition, which began in twelfth-century France, institutionalized torture across western Europe. Later, when Europeans set up overseas colonies, the Inquisition spread to the Americas, Asia, and Africa. The Roman Catholic Church, based in Rome, Italy, organized the Inquisition to root out heretics, or people who failed to show complete devotion to the teachings of the

COST OF DOING BUSINESS

Inquisitor Bernard Gui (*left, pictured here in a nineteenth-century engraving*) kept very accurate records of his interrogations and tortures, entering them in a book he titled the *Liber Sententiarum*, or *Book of Sentences*. (The book, bound in red leather, has survived the ages and is housed at the British Library in London.) An entry from 1323 records the cost of burning four heretics at the stake. Gui listed the price of wood, vines, and straw, which served as fuel for the fire; four stakes to which to tie the victims; ropes to tie them to the stakes; and the executioner's fee.

Catholic Church. The popes of the era appointed councils of church leaders to combat and punish heresy. Officials known as inquisitors employed torture to extract confessions from suspected heretics. Over several centuries, inquisitors targeted Protestants, Jews, Muslims, and others they regarded as a threat to the dominance of the Catholic Church. Victims were also targeted for behavior that had nothing to do with their religious beliefs. For instance, if a woman defied social norms by not getting married, she might be labeled a witch. During the Inquisition, tens of thousands of people, mostly women, were accused of witchcraft and executed—often by burning.

Perhaps the most notorious inquisitor was the French monk Bernard Gui (1260–1331), who over the course of about fifteen years oversaw the tortures of more than six hundred men and women—all of whom confessed to heresy under his interrogations. Gui's tortures, writes Durant, "took the form of flogging, burning, the rack, or solitary confinement in dark and narrow dungeons. The feet of the accused might be slowly roasted over burning coals; or he might be bound upon a triangular frame, and have his legs pulled by cords wound on a windlass [winch]."

Gui also employed a machine called the *garrucha*, the Spanish word for "pulley." The accused's hands were tied behind his or her back and attached to a rope. Using the garrucha, which was suspended from the ceiling, torturers then hoisted the victim off the ground. The pain experienced by the upper body could be horrific. No one subjected to the garrucha lasted more than a few minutes before admitting to anything Gui wanted to hear. Gui also used the tortures of the rack on his victims. He even wrote a manual for other inquisitors, titled *Conduct of Inquiry Concerning Heretical Depravity*.

Few people could endure the tortures of the inquisitors, and most readily confessed to being heretics. Afterward, courts of the era would mete out punishments—usually lengthy prison terms or executions. Methods of execution included burning at the stake and hanging.

WHIPS AND CHAINS

The Inquisition continued in the centuries after the Middle Ages, and tortures outside the realm of the Inquisition continued as well. During wartime, for example, governments used torture against spies and prisoners of war. During times of unrest, rulers used torture against revolutionaries within their own borders. Nations often used torture to keep conquered peoples from rebelling.

Some areas, including the North American colonies, allowed slavery, and slaves often endured cruel tortures at the hands of their masters. In his diaries of 1709 to 1712, Virginia plantation owner William Byrd II wrote about the punishments

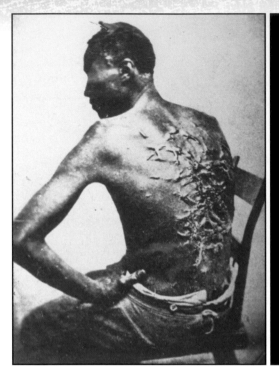

This photograph from 1863 shows an African American slave named Peter. His back bears the scars of repeated whippings by an overseer on the plantation where he worked in Louisiana.

he dispensed to his slaves, including putting bits (like those used on horses) or muzzles on their mouths to prevent them from talking and eating. When Byrd thought one slave was faking illness, he "put a branding iron on the place he [complained] of and put the bit on him." Whippings were also common. Solomon Northup, a slave in Louisiana in the 1840s and the 1850s, described to an interviewer the torturous punishments slaves could expect while picking cotton:

> When a new hand, one unaccustomed to the business, is sent for the first time into the field, he is whipped up smartly, and made for that day to pick as fast as he can possibly. At night [the cotton he has picked] is weighed, so that his capability to pick cotton is

known. He must bring in the same weight each night following. If it falls short, it is considered evidence that he has been laggard [lazy], and a greater or lesser number of lashes is the penalty.

In Russia, Czar Nicholas II (1868–1918) held onto power largely by ensuring that revolutionaries and other malcontents were removed from society. He either exiled them to the isolated, frozen landscape of Siberia in the far north or confined them to torture chambers in the bowels of his prisons.

In China during this era, criminals were sometimes placed outdoors in bamboo cages. The victim stood upright on a pile of stones or wooden planks, with his neck held tightly in a wooden frame at the top of the cage. Each day the torturers removed a plank or a stone from beneath the victim's feet, until he was finally left dangling by his neck. The victim died either of strangulation or a broken neck.

The Chinese employed another form of torture known as kneeling on chains. The victim was forced to kneel on heavy coiled chains, with his arms and legs bound to a wooden cross behind him. Eventually, over the course of days, this position forced the body's weight to shift onto the knees and toes. Eventually, over the course of days, the chain cut into the victim's knees, sometimes severing tendons and causing permanent disabilities.

TORTURES OF THE NAZIS

The twentieth century saw some of history's most barbaric cruelties. During World War II (1939–1945), no regime could match the Nazi government of Germany for savage tortures. The Nazis imprisoned in concentration camps Jews, Slavs, Roma (known then as Gypsies), homosexuals, intellectuals, artists, and others the Nazis regarded as undesirable. In the camps, millions of prisoners were systematically murdered, many with poisonous gas.

In addition, Nazi doctors stationed at the concentration camps used the large inmate population to perform medical experiments. At the Dachau camp, to simulate the hazards aviators faced when parachuting into the North Sea, doctors forced naked inmates to stay outside in freezing temperatures, sometimes even in freezing water, for up to fourteen hours at a time. At the Buchenwald camp, doctors frequently infected inmates with deadly diseases to test potential vaccines. At other camps, doctors experimented with the effects of mustard gas, a chemical that causes damage to the skin, eyes, and body organs. Some inmates were forced to inhale or drink the gas, while others were injected with it or had it forcibly rubbed into their wounds.

> "[Klaus Barbie] always carried a swagger stick, and . . . he tapped it all the time against his boots so that we could always tell he was coming to the cell. . . . It was absolute terror."
>
> —Lise Lesevre

The most notorious of the Nazi doctors was Josef Mengele, who conducted experiments at Auschwitz, the largest of the concentration camps. Like other Nazis, Mengele believed the inmates of the camp were inferior humans. He wanted to use science to prove their inferiority, so he collected blood, tissue samples, and even body organs to run tests. Mengele was very interested in the biological makeup of identical twins. At Auschwitz he experimented on three thousand sets of twins, most of them children. The test subjects underwent endless blood transfusions, as well as agonizing surgical operations and injections, administered without anesthesia. During this period of experimentation, test subjects were often starved.

In addition to inmates at concentration camps, the Nazis tortured other victims as well. In Germany and in German-occupied countries of Europe, the Gestapo, the Nazi's secret police force, arrested and tortured enemies of the regime. Prinz-Albrecht-Strasse 8, a former art school in Berlin, Germany, served as Gestapo headquarters. Thousands of victims were rounded up and tossed into cells in the building's basement, where they were tortured and often murdered.

Years after the Nazi defeat, stories of Nazi brutality continued to surface. Investigators spent decades tracking former Nazi leaders to bring them to justice. One was Klaus Barbie—known as the Butcher of Lyon (France)—who fled to South America after the war. In 1987 he was arrested and sent back to France to stand trial for the torture and murder of citizens of Lyon, where he had served as Gestapo chief during the Nazi occupation of France.

During Barbie's trial, a woman named Lise Lesevre, whom the Nazis had suspected of aiding the French Resistance against Nazi occupation, told of Barbie's tortures. She testified that Gestapo officers arrested her in 1943. In a Lyon jail cell, Gestapo officers held her head underwater in a bathtub, nearly drowning her. On another occasion, they tied her wrists, hoisted them over her head, and hung her from the ceiling until she lost consciousness. Barbie himself tortured her by striking her in the back with a spiked copper ball as she was held down by guards. "He was a savage," Lesevre said of Barbie. "He always carried a swagger stick, and when he had nothing to hit with it, he

In the Gulag, a system of prison camps that operated under Soviet dictator Joseph Stalin, prisoners frequently worked outdoors in bitter cold weather doing hard manual labor. They subsisted on near-starvation rations and often endured brutal tortures.

tapped it all the time against his boots so that we could always tell he was coming to the cell by the sound of the tapping that preceded him. . . . You had the feeling that a ferocious beast was coming into the cell. It was absolute terror." After a two-month trial, Barbie was convicted of war crimes and sentenced to life imprisonment. He died in prison in 1991.

STALIN'S PRISONS

The Soviet Union (a union of fifteen republics that included Russia) was an ally of the United States, Great Britain, and other European nation in helping to defeat Germany in World War II. The Soviet premier, Joseph Stalin, was a ruthless dictator who tolerated no dissent in his own country. During his rule, from 1928 to 1953, he ordered the arrest and imprisonment of millions of Soviet citizens. Stalin authorized the Soviet secret police force, known as the People's Commissariat for Internal Affairs (in Russian, the Narodnyy Komissariat Vnutrennikh Del, or NKVD), to enforce his rule domestically and internationally through violent and repressive measures. The NKVD had people arrested, tortured, and murdered. Some arrestees were sentenced to perform hard labor in the Gulag, a system of Soviet prison camps.

One victim of the Stalin regime was Aleksandr I. Solzhenitsyn. While serving in the Soviet army during World War II, Solzhenitsyn criticized Stalin's leadership and war strategy in private letters mailed home to a friend—never realizing that Stalin's spies were monitoring his mail. Stalin refused to tolerate even the private grumblings of a frontline soldier, and Solzhenitsyn was arrested just three months before the end of the war. He spent the next eleven years in what he called the Gulag Archipelago. (*Archipelago* is a geographical term for a cluster of islands scattered across a region. In like manner, the camps of the Soviet Gulag were scattered across remote areas of the Soviet Union.) In the Gulag, political prisoners worked building roads and railways, toiled in mines, and felled timber. They subsisted on near-starvation rations and were often tortured. Prisoners were crowded into tiny boxes, cells, and pits and often denied food and water. Guards sometimes tortured prisoners by preventing them from falling asleep, forcing them to stand with their eyes open. Prisoners singled out for punishment were sent to special cells. Solzhenitsyn describes the typical Gulag punishment cell:

> *No matter how hard it was in the ordinary cell, the*
> *punishment cells were always worse. And on return*
> *from there the ordinary cell always seemed like*

*paradise. In the punishment cell a human being was
systematically worn down by starvation and also,
usually, by cold. . . .*

*The prisoner was forced to undress down to his
underwear, and sometimes to his undershorts, and
he was forced to spend from three to five days in
the punishment cell without moving (since it was so
confining). He received hot gruel on the third day,
only. For the first few minutes you were convinced that
you'd not be able to last an hour. But, by some miracle,
a human being would indeed sit it out his five days,
perhaps acquiring in the course of it an illness that
would last him the rest of his life.*

After Solzhenitsyn was finally released in 1953, he wrote
a series of books about the Soviet Gulag and was awarded
the Nobel Prize in Literature in 1970. His most famous work,
The Gulag Archipelago, was published in 1973. It records the
history and horrors of the Soviet labor camps through personal
and eyewitness accounts, as well as through painstaking
historical research.

CHAPTER TWO

Torture Endures

Shot down in 1967 over Hanoi, North Vietnam, during the Vietnam War (1957–1975), US Navy pilot John McCain (later a US senator and presidential candidate) broke both legs and an arm as he parachuted out of his jet. He found little mercy from his captors, who allowed him to suffer from his injuries for several days before agreeing to hospitalize him. But even in the hospital, he received minimal treatment for his wounds. He grew thin and sick.

After several weeks in the hospital, McCain was transferred to Hoa Lo prison in Hanoi, sarcastically called the Hanoi Hilton by members of the US military imprisoned there. Prison life was cruel and spartan. McCain was held in solitary confinement for two years. Food was scarce. Moreover, McCain was regularly interrogated by North Vietnamese intelligence officers, anxious to learn what he knew about US military strategy. In the course of his interrogations, McCain was bound with ropes and beaten every two hours. He later wrote about several incidents of torture at the hands of an interrogator he nicknamed the Bug.

I sometimes sat on the stool looking into the cockeyed stare of the Bug. If I refused Bug's demands or gave him any lip, he would order guards to knock me around until I at least stopped trading insults with him. The Bug was a sadist. Or at least his hate for us was so irrational that it drove him to sadism. He was famous for accusing prisoners, when our recalcitrance [silence] enraged him, of killing his mother. Given the wildness of his rage, I often feared that we had.

On occasions when he was particularly determined, I would find myself trussed up and left for hours in ropes, my biceps bound tightly with several loops to cut off my circulation and the end of the rope cinched behind my back, pulling my shoulders and elbows unnaturally close together. It was incredibly painful.

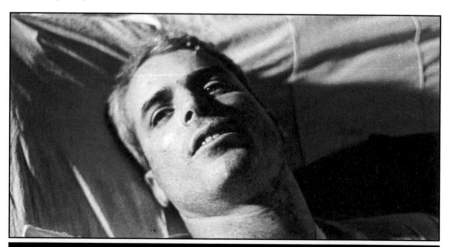

John McCain was photographed in a North Vietnamese hospital in 1967 after his jet was shot down during the Vietnam War. He was transferred to a prison camp, where he endured torture over the course of his six-year imprisonment.

McCain's vicious treatment at the hands of his North Vietnamese captors led him to despair, and he attempted suicide. Eventually he signed a fake confession, later commenting, "I had learned what we all learned over there: Every man has his breaking point. I had reached mine."

TWENTY-FIRST-CENTURY TORTURE

While torture is common in wartime, human rights groups report that it is also a fact of life in many parts of the twenty-first-century world. For example, defectors from North Korea tell horrific tales of torture in the prisons of dictator Kim Jong-un, the nation's leader since 2011, and in those of his predecessors. As many as two hundred thousand North Koreans are believed to be imprisoned and routinely tortured in this Asian nation. North Korean citizens can be jailed for watching foreign-made DVDs; criticizing Kim; or even just leaving dust on his portrait, which is prominently displayed around the nation. Guards sometimes burn prisoners and force them to eat rats and mice. Some sadistic guards order inmates to eat live rodents.

In North Korea, entire families are often held liable for the transgressions of one family member, so the children of suspected traitors or troublemakers may be held in custody as well. Additionally, many detainees are children born in prison camps to imprisoned mothers.

One of these child detainees was Shin Dong-hyuk, who spent the first twenty-three years of his life in a North Korean prison camp. He grew up eating scraps of food and witnessing tortures and abuses committed against other inmates. Occasionally he was tortured himself. According to Shin, he endured his first torture at the age of thirteen. "I was taken to a chamber full of all kinds of torture instruments," he recalls. "I was stripped, my

North Korea has one of the most repressive governments on Earth, with as many as two hundred thousand citizens kept imprisoned. Defectors say that torture is commonplace in North Korean prison camps. The woman in this photo stands guard at a prison camp on the banks of the Yalu River.

legs were cuffed and my hands were tied with rope. I was then hung by my legs and hands from the ceiling. Someone started a charcoal fire and brought it just under my back. I felt the heat at my waist and shrieked. My torturers pierced me with a steel hook near the groin to stop me writhing; the pain was so much that I fainted."

In Africa torture is common in nations such as Tanzania, Cameroon, and Zimbabwe. In 2007 a former agent of the secret police force of Robert Mugabe, Zimbabwe's brutal dictator since 1980, stepped forward to describe typical sessions of torture in which he participated. The man was interviewed after fleeing Zimbabwe, but he kept his name and exact location secret, fearing that Mugabe's police would try to find him. This is what he told a reporter:

> A man was put in the room for "random beating"—where you beat someone haphazardly, no

one really takes charge. You just beat him.

At first the guy was blocking [to protect his body from the blows]. *But we kept on kicking and assaulting him. After he started bleeding, we stopped.*

[Our officers] *said: "Why are you stopping?" So we had to keep on beating him. . . .*

Then another guy was brought in. They said he was a cattle rustler who had been sentenced to 35 years in prison.

He was put on a desk, and we were given rubber and sticks to beat his feet.

His feet turned black. When we removed him, he couldn't walk. He just fell down and collapsed.

Then a third guy came in. They said this guy had raped and killed a 13-year-old girl. We were told to apply electronic shocking.

We poured some water on him, and then each one of us applied the shock. That was it. By the time we left, he smelled of burnt meat. He just fell down on his face.

The fourth guy, we weren't told why he was brought in. A first-aid box was opened—and inside were pliers and screwdrivers. We asked the man to choose between the two.

Our captain attacked his ears with the pliers, pinching a piece out of it. He started bleeding heavily. He then reached into the box, took the [tape], *and put it over the man's mouth so that he couldn't make any noise. You could only see tears.*

Some Middle Eastern nations have a history of torturing citizens. For example, before he was ousted from power in 2003, Iraqi president Saddam Hussein used torture to silence dissidents during his decades-long rule. Dictators in Bahrain and the United Arab Emirates also rely on torture to maintain control in their countries. And torture is practiced in Saudi Arabia as well. In 2001 Ron Jones, a British tax adviser, visited the Saudi Arabian capital of Riyadh on business. There he was injured by a bomb blast set off by a terrorist. While recovering in a Riyadh hospital, Jones was arrested and accused of being

GAY RIGHTS ACTIVIST TORTURED

According to Amnesty International, homosexual behavior is a crime in thirty-eight African countries. In many African nations, activists who fight for gay rights are tortured. One was journalist and gay rights activist Eric Ohena Lembembe of Cameroon (right), who was found murdered in his home in July 2013. His neck and feet had been broken, and his hands, face, and feet had been burned with a hot iron. Gay rights activists suspect that Lembembe was tortured and killed by government agents. By 2014 not a single arrest had been made in the Lembembe torture-murder case.

Said Neela Ghoshal of the international group Human Rights Watch, "We don't know who killed Eric Lembembe, or why he was killed, but one thing is clear: the Cameroonian authorities' utter failure to stem homophobic [antigay] violence sends the message that these attacks can be carried out with impunity [without punishment]."

part of the terrorist ring that had planned the blast. He spent sixty-seven days in custody and was regularly tortured through physical abuse and sleep deprivation.

"They punched me, kicked me, bounced me off the walls," Jones recalls. "Then the caning [beating] started. They caned the soles of my feet and then they started caning my hands, sometimes with a pickaxe handle. They told me they arrested my wife and son and that they were doing this to them as well." During his time in custody, captors gave Jones doses of the drug Rohypnol, which left him in a stupor for about a week.

TELEVISING TORTURE VICTIMS

In the modern era, regimes have found television to be an important partner in torture. Authorities have not televised in-progress torture, but after a victim's will has been broken, authorities sometimes televise confessions to strike fear into the hearts of others. The technique is meant to terrify anyone who might have plans to protest against the government or to organize a coup (government overthrow).

Leaders in Iran frequently use this tactic. According to Darius Rejali, an Iranian-born professor of political science at Reed College in Portland, Oregon, authorities in Iran routinely employ sleep deprivation, electrical shocks, beatings, and floggings against political opponents. After a victim's will is broken, television cameras record the person's confession, which is then broadcast on nationwide television. "The government now [seeks] to make political opponents offer dramatic, seemingly voluntary, television recantations [retractions of earlier statements, in this case antigovernment remarks] to demoralize the opposition," says Rejali.

The Islamist terrorist group al-Qaeda was responsible for the September 11, 2001, attacks that killed about three thousand people in the United States. The group has used television since then to send a clear message to Americans that al-Qaeda continues to work actively against the United States. For example, in 2013 the group released a video of a seventy-two-year-old hostage, American Warren Weinstein, whom al-Qaeda kidnappers had snatched off a street in Pakistan in 2011. Weinstein had been working for a company hired by the US Agency for International Development—an aid organization that al-Qaeda opposes—to help Pakistanis escape poverty. The

DRUGGING AND TORTURE

Often interrogators and other torturers drug prisoners to confuse them, put them into a stupor, or make them more pliable and ready to talk. During World War II, Nazi torturers injected suspected spies and subversives with a drug called scopolamine. The drug puts users into zombielike trances, robbing them of their free will and making them very willing to answer questions.

In the years since World War II, interrogators have experimented with other drugs, including the mind-altering drug lysergic acid diethylamide, or LSD. When used in interrogations, LSD places users in a vulnerable state, making them willing to believe anything they are told. When threatened while under the influence of LSD, prisoners become very pliable in the hands of their torturers.

A common street drug, methamphetamine turns prisoners into chatterboxes. Another drug, pipradrol, places prisoners in a highly emotional state. Prisoners under the influence of pipradrol become nervous and animated, and they lack self-control, making them more likely to talk. Interrogators also administer doses of Ritalin, a stimulant. The drug can place prisoners in a euphoric state, making them willing to talk with little prompting.

video was aired internationally on dozens of TV news outlets. It showed Weinstein, looking haggard and weary, pleading with US officials to negotiate his release and to free several al-Qaeda members held in detention by the United States.

In the video, Weinstein said, "In order to alleviate my pain and suffering and to help me to reestablish my health, I have asked my captors if they will allow my family to visit me. They have agreed to do so, but they have done so on the basis that you will make an agreement, an arrangement with them that will provide a quid pro quo [exchange] with respect to their people who are being held as prisoner."

Although al-Qaeda leader Ayman al-Zawahiri maintained that his group had not tortured Weinstein, he was clearly under duress. In the video, he talked about the "pain and suffering" he had endured in captivity. Mike Baker, a former officer with the US Central Intelligence Agency (CIA), suggested that Weinstein may not have been physically tortured but may have endured psychological abuse, such as solitary confinement or constant threats of physical harm. Baker says, "This is psychological torture [against Weinstein] being performed by al-Qaeda, frankly. And they're doing this because . . . they're looking for publicity." With rare exceptions, the United States does not negotiate with terrorist groups, so as of early 2014, Weinstein was still in the custody of al-Qaeda.

OUTSIDE THE LAW

Drug kingpins and other criminals also use torture to strike fear in their enemies, extract information, and exact revenge. In a book describing a gangland murder, an American Mafia insider, identified only as Joey, tells of the kidnappings of two thieves—Manny and Allie—caught stealing from the mob. The mob suspected that someone was giving Manny and Allie inside information, so gangsters known as button men took the two thieves to a funeral home basement to find out what they knew. Joey says:

> It's not that Manny and Allie wanted to play hero and protect their silent partner, it's just that they took one look around, saw the empty coffins, and figured they were going to have a bad case of death as soon as they told everything they knew. So they were in no particular hurry to talk.
>
> Therefore, it was up to the buttonmen to (a) convince them they would not be hurt if they told everything they knew, or (b) convince them that being dead could actually be better than being alive. The buttonmen opted for alternative b. They used some very subtle techniques. It is a well-known fact in funeral-home basements that you can hurt a guy pretty good by poking his [genitals] with an ice pick. Pins inserted directly under the fingernails also prove very persuasive. This was demonstrated to Allie and Manny and they showed a willingness to talk. And, as soon as they stopped screaming, they did.

TORTURE IN THE DRUG WAR

Certainly, Manny and Allie were aware of the dangers of stealing from mobsters. Their torturers made them pay a painful price. Yet criminals also torture innocent victims. One example was María Santos Gorrostieta Salazar, the mayor of the small Mexican town of Tiquicheo. Gorrostieta Salazar had waged a campaign against drug gangs in her town. In 2012, in full public

PSYCHOLOGICAL TORTURE

Some forms of torture do not leave physical scars. For example, threats of rape, forcing victims to watch others undergo torture, and telling prisoners they will be executed or their loved ones will be killed are forms of psychological torture. These can be just as stressful as physical abuse.

In 2007 researchers at King's College in London interviewed 279 torture victims. Using a scale of 1 to 4, they asked victims to rate the stress created by various tortures. The results show that victims of psychological torture experienced degrees of stress similar to those suffered by victims of physical abuse. For example, victims who were burned on parts of their bodies recorded an average stress level of 3.6. Those who were threatened with rape but not raped also reported an average stress level of 3.6. Those forced to witness the tortures of others reported a similar stress level of 3.4.

view, armed gunmen stopped her car, dragged her out, took her into their car, and drove off. Later, the body of the thirty-six year-old mother of three was found beaten, bruised, and stabbed—evidence that she had been tortured before she was murdered. Clearly, the drug gangs wanted to send a message to other public officials to stay out of the way of the illegal narcotics business.

In retaliation, Mexican police have also used torture as a weapon, extracting confessions from drug traffickers. In 2011 the international research and advocacy group Human Rights Watch (HRW) issued a report revealing that Mexican police officers and army soldiers had engaged in at least 170 cases of torture against suspected drug traffickers. In some cases, innocent people caught up in police dragnets found themselves enduring torture at the hands of the authorities. According to HRW, techniques included beatings, mock executions, threats of rape, electric shocks, and near asphyxiation with plastic bags. The report cited the case of one arrestee, Marcelo Laguarda Dávila, who in 2010 was abducted, interrogated, and tortured by police officers until he confessed to drug trafficking charges. Said Laguarda Dávila after his experience, "They took a cloth and they wrapped it around my head except for my nose. Later I learned that this was what they called 'the mummy.' They left me like this and began to do the thing with the water [waterboarding, or pouring water into a prisoner's nose and mouth] . . . the water came in directly through my nose. They repeated this three times. That's when I said, 'That's it, I'll confess to whatever you want.'"

But Laguarda Dávila had no involvement in Mexico's illegal drug trade. The police officers had tortured an innocent man.

ABU GHRAIB

The United States has had its own torture scandals. During the Iraq War (2003–2011), Americans were shocked to learn of the widespread torture of enemy prisoners held by the US military at Abu Ghraib prison in Iraq.

The first evidence of torture at Abu Ghraib surfaced in late 2003, when a US soldier reported instances of prisoner abuse at the facility. In the spring of 2004, photos of abused prisoners were leaked to the press. Photos showed appalling scenes of sexual humiliation and physical abuse, with smiling US military guards standing by. In one photo, a female guard mocked naked male prisoners. In another she held a prisoner on a leash like a dog. One prisoner died after being beaten and suspended by his wrists with his hands tied behind his back. In this position, he was unable to breathe. In 2004 US Army general Antonio Taguba released a report of his investigation of prisoner abuse at Abu Ghraib. Taguba's lengthy report revealed a litany of instances of torture at the jail, including the following:

Prisoners at Abu Ghraib were forced to stand in stress positions for hours at a time. Using such tactics, prison authorities hoped to weaken, demoralize, and dishearten prisoners so they would be more likely to confess to or implicate others in terrorist activities.

- *Beating detainees with a broom handle and a chair*
- *Punching, slapping, and kicking detainees and jumping on their bare feet*
- *Pouring freezing cold water on naked detainees*
- *Threatening detainees with a 9mm pistol*
- *Attaching wires to a prisoner's fingers, toes, and penis to simulate electric torture*
- *Using dogs to frighten and in one instance bite a detainee*

- *The rape, by a member of the army military police, of a female detainee*
- *Threatening male detainees with rape*
- *Sodomizing a detainee*
- *Videotaping and photographing naked male and female detainees*
- *Forcibly arranging detainees in sexually explicit positions for photographing*
- *Arranging naked male detainees in a pile and then jumping or sitting on them*
- *Keeping detainees naked for several days at a time*
- *Forcing naked male detainees to wear women's underwear*
- *Placing a dog chain around a naked detainee's neck*

"It was humiliating," said one of the Abu Ghraib detainees, Hayder Sabbar Abd. "We did not think that we would survive. All of us believed we would be killed and not get out alive." Eventually, eleven members of the US military were convicted of criminal charges associated with the abuse of prisoners. Two soldiers, Charles Graner and Lynndie England—said to be the ringleaders among the abusive guards—were sentenced to lengthy prison terms.

Although no high-level officers were charged with crimes, critics said that responsibility for the abuse went all the way up the military chain of command to the commander in chief, President George W. Bush. The Bush administration had authorized the use of harsh interrogation techniques for war prisoners, creating an atmosphere in which torture was tolerated and even encouraged. After the torture at Abu Ghraib was revealed, critics called for the resignation of US secretary of defense Donald Rumsfeld, and Congress held hearings to investigate the abuse.

For a nation with a long history of the defense of justice, in particular the Eighth Amendment of the US Constitution, which forbids cruel and unusual punishment, the revelations at Abu Ghraib were shocking. Many Americans thought the United States and its military personnel were above such reprehensible tactics. But in the face of mountains of evidence from a variety of sources, both domestic and international, there was no denying that guards at Abu Ghraib had been abusive—and that those in positions of authority had condoned the abuse and torture. Reflecting the viewpoint of many people around the world, Mohamed Kamal, a professor of political science at Cairo University in Egypt, said, "Eventually, the images will fade away, but it will be very difficult for the US to [continue to effectively] preach democracy and respect for human rights."

> There was no denying that guards at Abu Ghraib had been abusive—and that those in positions of authority had condoned the abuse and torture.

"INDUSTRIAL" KILLING IN SYRIA

In the Middle Eastern nation of Syria, civil war erupted in 2011, with opposition fighters attempting to overthrow the government of dictator Bashar al-Assad. Since the conflict began, more than 160,000 people have died and millions have had to flee their homes.

In his effort to defeat the opposition, Assad has frequently resorted to torture. The widespread nature of that torture became evident in the spring of 2014 when a military-police photographer broke with Syrian forces and smuggled fifty-five thousand digital images out of Syria. The pictures, which were presented to the United Nations Security Council that April, showed eleven thousand dead detainees. They had endured gruesome tortures at the hands of Assad's security forces. Prisoners had been beaten, strangled, and starved to death. Some victims had had their eyes gouged out. Others showed signs of electrocution.

Samantha Power, US ambassador to the United Nations, condemned the torture. The photos, she said, "indicate that the Assad regime has carried out systematic, widespread and industrial killing. Nobody who sees these images will ever be the same."

CHAPTER THREE

The Push for Human Rights

In the early 1700s, Europe entered the Enlightenment—an era in which philosophers and scientists emphasized reason, evidence, and scientific method over historical tradition and religious faith. During the Enlightenment, artists and thinkers made great advances in the sciences and the arts. Leaders of the Enlightenment believed that people should rely on knowledge to improve the human condition and to expand their understanding of the universe.

By then European colonies had been established in North America. Many leading citizens of those colonies, among them future US presidents John Adams and Thomas Jefferson and statesman Benjamin Franklin, were proponents of the Enlightenment. All read and embraced the message of a treatise called *Of Crimes and Punishments*, written by eighteenth-century Italian jurist Cesare Beccaria. Beccaria wrote about the prevailing views of the time: "The torture of a criminal while his trial is being put together is a cruelty accepted by most nations, whether to compel him to confess a crime, to exploit the contradictions he runs into, to uncover his accomplices . . .

or, lastly, to expose other crimes of which he is guilty but with which he has not been charged." He presented various arguments against torture and noted the many "examples of innocent persons who, from the agony of torture, have confessed themselves guilty."

Following the American Revolution (1775–1783), the founders of the United States drafted the US Constitution, which specifically guarantees fair and public trials. The Eighth Amendment to the Constitution, ratified in 1791, outlaws torture by prohibiting cruel and unusual punishment.

Other countries took similar steps. In postrevolutionary France, in the late 1700s, General Napoleon Bonaparte (later emperor) decreed that torture was a cruel practice and prohibited its use. "The barbarous custom of having men beaten who are suspected of having important secrets to reveal must be abolished," he declared. By then, many more European countries had banned torture. Among them were Sweden, Prussia, Denmark, Austria, the Netherlands, Norway, Portugal, and Switzerland. Even Spain, where the Inquisition endured until 1834, eventually banned torture.

INALIENABLE RIGHTS

In the Western world, the movement toward abolishing torture was part of a much wider recognition of democratic principles and human rights. US lawmakers encoded the basic rights and freedoms of citizens in the first ten amendments to the US Constitution, collectively known as the Bill of Rights.

Inspired by the American experience of fighting for self-rule, France fought its own revolution (1789–1799) to overthrow its monarchy. A key French document of that revolution was the *Declaration of the Rights of Man and of the Citizen*, published in 1789. The document states that all people have the right to liberty, property, security, and freedom from oppression. It also describes the limitations of government and the obligations of citizens in a free society.

This painting by Jean-Jacques François Le Barbier, made in 1793, contains the French text of the *Declaration of the Rights of Man and of the Citizen*, as well as symbols that promote the ideals of democracy and human rights. The broken chain represents the end of the French monarchy, which was seen as having shackled the French people. The scepter of power, held by the winged figure, is being transferred to common citizens.

The push for human rights made its way to the battlefield as well. In the late 1850s, Swiss businessman Henri Dunant was appalled by the plight of soldiers wounded in battle and left to die. In 1863 Dunant founded the International Committee of the Red Cross and also organized a conference in Geneva, Switzerland, to establish rules for the humane conduct of war. Attendees drafted a treaty declaring that hospitals and medics could operate on the battlefield with neutral status—that is, that they wouldn't be fired upon by enemy forces. In 1864 twelve countries signed the treaty, which came to be called the First Geneva Convention. The United States signed the treaty in 1882.

During the conference in Geneva, the United States was embroiled in its bloody Civil War (1861–1865), fought between the South and the North, primarily over slavery. Shortly after the war, in December 1865, the US Congress ratified the Thirteenth Amendment to the Constitution, abolishing slavery.

> **Henri Dunant ... organized a conference in Geneva, Switzerland, to establish rules for the humane conduct of war. Attendees drafted a treaty declaring that hospitals and medics could operate on the battlefield with neutral status.**

In the twentieth century, Europe was decimated by the horrors of World War I (1914–1918), in which new military technologies killed millions of people. The devastation led to deep introspection and to an international call to work for peace and human rights. Several countries formed the League of Nations in 1919. The organization's mission was to resolve international disputes before they erupted into warfare. Although the United States did not join the league,

Following the creation of the International Red Cross in 1863, the American Red Cross was formed in 1881. The organization sent nurses such as this one to work in Europe during World War I. As put forth in the First Geneva Convention, medical personnel were allowed to care for wounded soldiers during the war without fear of being fired upon by the enemy.

which eventually collapsed, the league did adopt provisions recognizing human rights, including the rights of women and the rights of workers to organize labor unions.

CONVENTIONS AGAINST TORTURE

The League of Nations did not eradicate war, however, and as World War II came to a close, the notion of forming a group to resolve international disputes was resurrected. In June 1945, fifty nations sent representatives to a meeting in San Francisco, California, to draw up a charter for the United Nations (UN). With the horrors of the Nazi regime in mind—the murders, enslavement, and torture of millions of innocent Europeans—the delegates in San Francisco resolved to make the United Nations into a powerful institution that would advocate for world peace, cooperation, and human rights.

SELECTIONS FROM THE FIRST GENEVA CONVENTION

Some of the key points in the First Geneva Convention of the mid-nineteenth century cover the treatment of hospital staff and wounded or sick combatants in wartime.

- **Article 1:** "Ambulances and military hospitals shall be recognized as neutral, and as such, protected and respected by the belligerents [warring parties] as long as they accommodate wounded and sick...."

- **Article 2:** "Hospital and ambulance personnel, including the quarter-master's staff, the medical, administrative and transport services, and the chaplains, shall have the benefit of the same neutrality when on duty, and while there remain any wounded to be brought in or assisted."

- **Article 6:** "Wounded or sick combatants, to whatever nation they may belong, shall be collected and cared for.... Evacuation parties, and the personnel conducting them, shall be considered as being absolutely neutral."

- **Article 7:** "A distinctive and uniform flag shall be adopted for hospitals, ambulances and evacuation parties. It should in all circumstances be accompanied by the national flag. An armlet may also be worn by personnel enjoying neutrality but its issue shall be left to the military authorities. Both flag and armlet shall bear a red cross on a white ground."

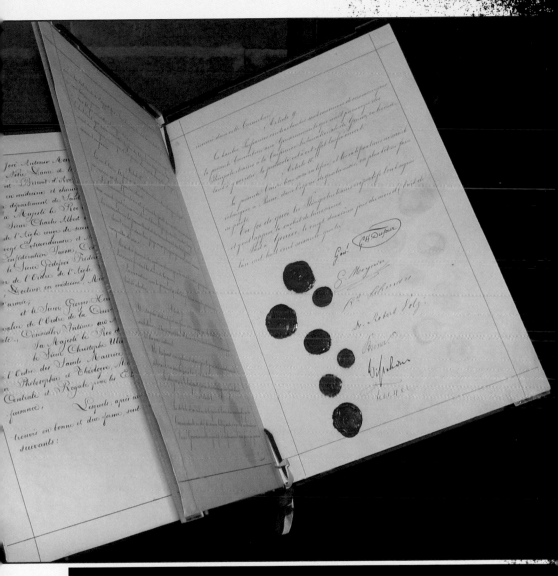

The original manuscript of the First Geneva Convention is on display at the International Red Cross and Red Crescent Museum in Geneva. In the 1860s, when the convention was signed, it was customary to make impressions in wax to authenticate signatures on official documents. The signers of the convention pressed their seals into red wax next to their signatures.

In 1946, one year after the UN was formed, delegates voted to establish the UN Commission on Human Rights (UNCHR). The commission was charged with investigating human rights abuses committed by governments and with forming policies to protect human rights. Toward that end, the commission drafted the Universal Declaration of Human Rights, which was adopted in 1948. Article 5 of the declaration prohibits torture. It states, "No one shall be subjected to torture or to cruel, inhuman or degrading treatment or punishment." Eleanor Roosevelt, the widow of US president Franklin D. Roosevelt, was a strong advocate for human rights. She chaired the UN committee that drafted the declaration.

Former first lady Eleanor Roosevelt holds a copy of the Universal Declaration of Human Rights. The 1948 document was printed in multiple languages, including English, French, and Spanish. Since then, the document has been translated into 438 different languages, including sign language.

By then the First Geneva Convention had been expanded, with additional provisions added in 1906 and 1929. More rules were added in 1949 and 1977. Together, these agreements established the humanitarian treatment of wounded and sick soldiers, prisoners of war, and civilians during wartime. These rules also banned torture. The United Nations took on the job of enforcing the Geneva Conventions.

The UN took additional measures against torture in the late twentieth century. The most important of these was the Convention against Torture and Other Cruel, Inhuman or Degrading Treatment or Punishment, passed in 1984 and taking effect in 1987. The convention defined torture as follows:

> For the purposes of this Convention, the term "torture" means any act by which severe pain or suffering, whether physical or mental, is intentionally inflicted on a person for such purposes as obtaining from him or a third person information or a confession, punishing him for an act he or a third person has committed or is suspected of having committed, or intimidating or coercing him or a third person, or for any reason based on discrimination of any kind, when such pain or suffering is inflicted by or at the instigation of or with the consent or acquiescence of a public official or other person acting in an official capacity. It does not include pain or suffering arising only from, inherent in or incidental to lawful sanctions.

More than 150 countries, including the United States, have signed the measure.

At a 2001 demonstration in Washington, DC, protesters denounced human-rights abuses by government-backed paramilitary groups in Colombia and demanded closure of the School of the Americas, where some of the Colombian fighters had been trained. The Death of Negotiations sign refers to failed peace negotiations in Colombia.

CHAPTER FOUR

Blood on American Hands

While the United States was signing on to international anti-torture conventions, the US Department of Defense (DOD) was operating a secret institution known as the School of the Americas (SOA). Established in 1946, the school operated first in Panama in Central America and in 1984 was moved to Fort Benning, Georgia.

At the school, members of the CIA and US military taught harsh techniques of arrest and interrogation designed to extract information from foreign spies and terrorists. These techniques included early-morning capture to maximize shock, immediate hooding and blindfolding of captives, forced nudity and other forms of humiliation, sensory deprivation (depriving prisoners of sights, sounds, and other sensations that orient humans in space and time), sensory overload (such as blasting prisoners with loud music or bright lights), denial of sleep and food, imprisonment in environments of extreme heat and cold, isolation, stress positions, and physical abuse.

The justification for establishing the SOA and for the harsh measures taught at the school could be found in the rubble of the US Navy base at Pearl Harbor, Hawaii. On December 7, 1941, the Japanese military made a surprise attack on the base, killing more than two thousand Americans and propelling the United States to enter World War II.

In the aftermath of the attack, US military leaders concluded that it might have been thwarted had they had better intelligence. Says Willard C. Matthias, a former analyst for the CIA, "The Japanese attack on Pearl Harbor on Sunday, December 7, 1941, changed America's thinking about its role in the world. . . . One of the major military steps undertaken in the United States was to strengthen the intelligence-gathering and intelligence-analysis capability of the military services." Vowing to never be caught by surprise again, the DOD established the School of the Americas.

THE CIA'S TORTURE MANUAL

By the early 1960s, the United States was fully engaged in a conflict known as the Cold War (1945–1991). Desperate to limit the Soviet Union's influence in the Western Hemisphere, the US government and military leaders went to extreme measures to ensure American geopolitical dominance. Because the Soviet Union had a Communist government, many US efforts during the era went to battling Communism around the globe through propaganda, proxy wars, and covert operations.

In 1959 the island nation of Cuba fell to a revolutionary band led by Fidel Castro. He set up a Communist government in Cuba, with backing from the Soviet Union, giving the Soviets a foothold just 90 miles (145 kilometers) from the US mainland. In Washington, DC, nervous political leaders wanted assurances that the Soviets would find no more allies in Latin America. They invited police and military officers from Latin America to attend the SOA to learn how to root out Communists in their countries.

At the school, instructors used "torture manuals," written by the CIA and the US military, providing specifics on how to extract information from suspects using physically abusive methods. "While we do not stress the use of coercive techniques, we do want to make you aware of them and the proper way

When Fidel Castro *(center)* and his guerrilla army set up a Communist government in Cuba, US military and political leaders were alarmed. Hoping to prevent other Communist revolutions in the Western Hemisphere, instructors at the School of the Americas taught torture techniques to Latin American military and police officers.

to use them," one manual said. It went on to explain methods for applying extreme heat and cold to detainees, depriving them of sleep and food, forcing them to stand in painfully uncomfortable positions for long periods, and imprisoning them in solitary confinement. Such methods, the manual suggested, would "destroy [the] capacity to resist."

THE DIRTY WARS

Many historians say that tactics taught at the SOA did not help protect Americans from the perceived evils of Communism. Instead, the techniques made their way to cruel, repressive dictators, who used the methods to ensure a tight grip on power. In the late twentieth century, for example, a series of Latin American dictators waged "dirty wars," or campaigns of terror, against their own people, often using techniques taught at the SOA. Historians believe that during these campaigns, secret police forces in nations such as El Salvador, Guatemala, Nicaragua, Argentina, and Chile tossed hundreds of thousands of suspected dissidents into jails—some of them Communist sympathizers but also human rights activists, artists, journalists, and intellectuals. Prisoners were held without charges and were tortured. Many were murdered. Others are said to have disappeared—no one knows their exact fate.

In Chile, Communist-leaning Salvador Allende came to power in 1970 through a democratic election. Fearing that Allende would seek a political and economic ally in the Soviet Union, the CIA sponsored a coup to oust him. He was replaced by a US-backed dictator, Augusto Pinochet, who for seventeen years ruled Chile with an iron fist. For training, Pinochet sent many members of his secret police, the National Intelligence Directorate, to the SOA.

Guatemala too sent military officers and intelligence agents to the SOA. During the 1980s, the Guatemalan government waged its own dirty war against Guatemalan citizens, intent on stamping out Communist insurgents. Many innocent Guatemalans were brutally victimized by the relentless campaign of terror.

One victim of the dirty war in Guatemala was a twenty-seven-year-old US nun, Sister Dianna Ortiz, who lived to tell her story. Mistaken for a rebel fighter named Veronica Ortiz Hernandez, Sister Dianna was abducted in the Guatemalan town of Antigua, where she was teaching religion and literacy to young children in 1989. She was then spirited away to a secret prison, where torturers repeatedly pressed lit cigarettes into her flesh. She was held not in a cell but in an open pit where many captives had already died. Some of the bodies were children. Some had been brutally executed through decapitation. Rats nibbled at their corpses.

From time to time in her twenty-four-hour ordeal, the guards would lift Ortiz out of the pit for the purposes of interrogation—and to rape her. On one occasion, the guards put a knife in her hand and, using force to guide her hand, thrust the weapon into another prisoner, killing the woman instantly. She recalls, "At that point in my torture wanting to die, I did not resist. . . . What I remember is blood gushing—spurting like a water fountain—and my screams lost in the cries of the woman."

EXPOSED!

With the fall of the Soviet Union in 1991, the Cold War ended. The SOA switched its focus from fighting Communism to fighting the war on drugs in Latin America. In 1992 US secretary of defense Dick Cheney (who later served as vice president to George W. Bush) reviewed the SOA torture manuals. He called them objectionable and not in keeping with US policy. He ordered the school to stop using them.

For decades the torture manuals had been kept secret from the public. But US journalists learned about them and formally requested that the government release them. When the contents of the manuals were revealed in 1996, many Americans were

In 1990 a small group of activists formed SOA Watch, dedicated to shutting down the School of the Americas (whose name was changed to the Western Hemisphere Institute for Security Cooperation in 2000). The school says that it no longer teaches torture techniques. But critics are skeptical of this claim. They claim that graduates continue to use their training to violate human rights in their home countries. This photo from 2009 shows banners, signs, and crosses that protesters placed at the gates of the school in Fort Benning, Georgia.

outraged. Joseph P. Kennedy II, a US congressional representative from Massachusetts, called for closure of the School of the Americas. He compared the activities there to those of the Schutzstaffel, or SS, a notoriously brutal military unit established by the Nazi regime during World War II. "These tactics come right out of an SS manual and have no place in a civilized society," Kennedy said. "They certainly have no place in any course taught with taxpayer dollars on US soil by members of our own military." Despite criticism, the SOA remained open. In 2000 it changed its name to the Western Hemisphere Institute for Security Cooperation. The school continues to train soldiers and law enforcement officers from Latin America, but the school says that students are no longer trained in torture techniques.

TORTURE AND THE WAR ON TERRORISM

After the September 11, 2001, terrorist attacks, some Americans argued that torture was still a necessary tool in the fight against US enemies. Alan Dershowitz, a former professor at Harvard Law School, said at the time that when American lives are at stake, torture should be an acceptable tactic. He even mentioned specific forms of torture, such as inserting needles under fingernails. "I want maximal pain, minimum lethality," Dershowitz wrote. "You don't want [the damage] to be permanent, you don't want someone to be walking with a limp, but you want to cause the most excruciating, intense, immediate pain. . . . I [don't] want to be squeamish about it. People have asked me whether I would do the torturing and my answer is, yes, I would if I thought it could save a city from being blown up."

Soon after the 9/11 attacks, the administration of President George W. Bush reexamined US law and approved "enhanced interrogation" techniques that might help interrogators find those responsible for the attacks and develop intelligence to stop additional terrorist plots. These techniques included many tactics previously taught at the SOA. Guards at the US military prison at Guantanamo Bay, Cuba, and elsewhere used the methods on suspected terrorists captured in Afghanistan and Iraq in the so-called War on Terror.

A particularly gruesome technique used on detainees at Guantanamo was waterboarding. When a suspect is waterboarded, he is strapped to a stiff board. The suspect's head is wrapped in a towel. Water is poured onto his nose or mouth for several seconds. During that time, the suspect can't breathe and endures the sensation of drowning. Between pours, the subject is interrogated. Failure to answer a question results in another dowsing.

One terrorist captured after the 9/11 attacks—Khalid Sheikh Mohammed, the mastermind of the attacks—was reportedly waterboarded 183 times. In addition, he was stripped naked and forced to stand or squat in painfully uncomfortable positions

The September 11 terrorist attacks on the United States set off a debate about whether or not the use of torture was justified. Some argued that the 9/11 terrorists, who were not affiliated with traditional armies, were not entitled to the protections against torture guaranteed in the Geneva Conventions.

for hours. He was denied use of a toilet and was forced to wear a diaper. He was assaulted by his interrogators—shoved hard against the walls of his cell and slapped repeatedly.

Throughout his interrogation, Mohammed refused to talk. But his will was finally broken after 180 straight hours (almost eight days) without sleep. When he finally agreed to talk, Mohammed revealed all he knew about the 2001 terrorist attacks and those involved in the plot. He also revealed plans for other attacks on US cities. CIA interrogators said that Mohammed's confession helped them thwart plans by extremists to blow up airliners as they flew over West Coast cities.

When he finally agreed to talk, Mohammed revealed all he knew about the 2001 terrorist attacks and those involved in the plot. He also revealed plans for other attacks on US cities.

THE TICKING TIME BOMB

In subjecting Mohammed to abusive interrogation techniques, interrogators had in mind a "ticking time bomb" scenario—one in which thousands or millions of Americans would die if an active plot against the United States were not unearthed quickly. Alan Dershowitz believes that in such scenarios, torture is highly justified. He says, "If we ever had the ticking bomb case—somebody who we believed had plans with others who were out free to blow up a major city or plant a nuclear bomb—there's no question that the Americans would do everything they have to do to prevent it."

But others suggest that torture is ineffective, even in a ticking time bomb situation. Many experts say that people will say anything to escape the horrific pain of torture, and they won't necessarily tell the truth. They might give false information to buy time until the planned attack goes off. Says Ali Soufan, a former agent for the Federal Bureau of Investigation (FBI), "From my experience—and I speak as someone who has personally interrogated many terrorists and elicited important actionable intelligence—I strongly believe that it is a mistake to use what has become known as the 'enhanced interrogation techniques,' a position shared by many professional operatives."

> "[Informed interrogation] is not about being nice or soft.... It is about outwitting the detainee by using ... interpersonal, cognitive, and emotional strategies."
> —Ali Soufan, former FBI interrogator

INFORMED INTERROGATION

Instead of enhanced interrogation techniques, Soufan advocates the informed interrogation approach, which military and civilian intelligence officers have used successfully for decades. With this approach, the interrogator does not employ pain or the threat of pain. Instead, the interrogator works to establish trust with a detainee. Before the interrogation begins, the interviewer learns about the detainee and the detainee's country. During the interrogation, the interviewer uses that knowledge to forge a bond with the suspect.

Many detainees are held in solitary confinement, and the only human contact they have is with an interrogator. This puts the interrogator in a powerful position to gain the detainee's trust. "People crave human contact, and this is especially true in some cultures more than others," says Soufan. "The interrogator turns this knowledge into an advantage by becoming the one person the detainee can talk to and who listens to what he has to say, and uses this to encourage the detainee to open up."

The interrogator can use knowledge about the detainee to create an atmosphere of comfort. For instance, when Soufan interviewed Abu Zubaydah, an al-Qaeda leader, he recalls that "I asked him his name. He replied with his alias. I then asked him, 'How about if I call you Hani?' That was the name his mother nicknamed him as a child. He looked at me in shock, said 'OK,' and we started talking."

By developing bonds with detainees, Soufan maintains, interrogators can obtain much more information than if they resort to techniques such as waterboarding. Says Soufan, "[Informed interrogation] is not about being nice or soft. It is a knowledge-based approach. It is about outwitting the detainee by using a combination of interpersonal, cognitive, and emotional strategies to get the information needed. If done correctly it's an approach that works quickly and effectively because it outwits the detainee using a method that he is not trained, or able, to resist."

EXTRAORDINARY RENDITION

In the first decade of the 2000s, the United States abducted hundreds of foreign terror suspects. In a practice known as extraordinary rendition, the CIA sent some of these suspects to nations known for using brutal interrogation tactics. These countries—ruled by dictators with friendly relations with the United States—included Jordan, Egypt, Algeria, Djibouti, Malawi, Morocco, Pakistan, Somalia, and Saudi Arabia. The suspects provided information under torture—but the actual acts of torture were not committed by US agents. Said Alan Dershowitz, "We subcontract torture to [these nations] and they're very good at it."

PRO: TORTURE IS JUSTIFIED

"A terrorist is by profession, indeed by definition, an unlawful combatant: He lives outside the laws of war because he does not wear a uniform, he hides among civilians, and he deliberately targets innocents. He is entitled to no protections whatsoever. People seem to think that the postwar Geneva Conventions were written only to protect detainees. In fact, their deeper purpose was to provide a deterrent to the kind of barbaric treatment of civilians that had become so horribly apparent during the first half of the 20th century, and in particular, during the Second World War....

"Breaking the laws of war and abusing civilians are what, to understate the matter vastly, terrorists do for a living. They are entitled, therefore, to nothing. Anyone who blows up a car bomb in a market deserves to spend the rest of his life roasting on a spit over an open fire."

—Charles Krauthammer, Pulitzer Prize–winning political commentator and columnist, *Washington Post,* 2005

"Enter Khalid Sheikh Mohammed: our most valuable capture in our war on terror....His membership in Al Qaeda more or less rules out his 'innocence' in any important sense, and his rank in the organization suggests that his knowledge of planned atrocities must be extensive....If there is even one chance in a million that he will tell us something under torture that will lead to the further dismantling of Al Qaeda, it seems that we should use every means at our disposal to get him talking."

—Sam Harris, author, philosopher, and neuroscientist, 2004

CON: TORTURE CAN NEVER BE JUSTIFIED

"Nations that use torture disgrace themselves. Armed forces and police that torture inevitably become brutalized and corrupted. 'Limited' use of torture quickly becomes generalized. 'Information' obtained by torture is mostly unreliable. I learned these truths over fifty years covering dirty . . . wars, from Algeria to Indochina, Central and South America, southern Africa, the Mideast, Afghanistan, and Kashmir in which torture was commonly used. . . .

"When I served in the US Army, I was taught that any illegal order, even from the president, must be refused and that mistreating prisoners was a crime. President Obama must show the world that America upholds the law, rejects torture of all kinds, and that no officials are above the law. Otherwise, there is no other way to prevent the recurrence of torture in the future."

—Eric Margolis, award-winning syndicated journalist and author, 2009

"I don't know how many lives torture has saved, but I know how many torture has taken because we know this war [the Iraq War] was started and prosecuted with information gained through coercion and that produces such high unreliability that you're bound to make mistakes, kill innocent people, and lose your own soldiers. If people want good intelligence, torture is not the way to get it."

—Darius Rejali, author, scholar, and torture expert, 2014

A small-scale extraordinary rendition program had begun in the 1990s, during the presidency of Bill Clinton. After the 2001 terrorist attacks, the CIA significantly expanded the program. Four years after the attacks, the American Civil Liberties Union (ACLU) reported that at least 150 suspects had been sent to foreign countries for interrogation and were likely to have been tortured during questioning. By then the US Justice Department had issued an opinion supporting extraordinary rendition. It said that if prisoners were tortured in foreign countries, the United States was not legally responsible for their treatment. But the ACLU pointed out that extraordinary rendition was in violation of UN conventions against torture.

In 2009 a new US president, Barack Obama, took office. During the presidential campaign, Obama had said that he opposed the use of torture. Obama's Republican opponent, John McCain—by then a US senator from Arizona—took a similar position. Soon after taking office, Obama signed an executive order limiting the use of enhanced interrogation techniques. "Waterboarding is torture," Obama insisted. "It's contrary to America's traditions. It's contrary to our ideals. That's not who we are. That's not how we operate. We don't need it in order to prosecute the war on terrorism. And we did the right thing by ending that practice. If we want to lead around the world, part of our leadership is setting a good example."

Despite Obama's stance on waterboarding, critics say that the US military continues to use torture techniques on prisoners. For instance, prisoners at Guantanamo Bay have staged hunger strikes to protest what they see as their unlawful detention. In response, guards at the prison strap them to chairs twice a day, insert feeding tubes down their throats and noses, and force nutritional fluids into their bodies. Guards also force

Several times since 2005, inmates at the US military prison at Guantanamo Bay, Cuba, have organized hunger strikes to protest their detention. To keep the strikers from starving, guards strap them down, force-feed them, and also force them to take laxative medications, a process that many decry as torture.

laxative medications down prisoners' throats and then, after they defecate, leave them sitting in their own waste for several hours. This practice is designed to humiliate the prisoners and convince them to give up their hunger strikes. Amnesty International and many other groups decry the practice as torture.

At Tuol Sleng prison, as many as twenty thousand Cambodians were tortured and killed during the Khmer Rouge dictatorship. In 1980 the prison was turned into a museum to honor and memorialize the victims. Ing Pech, one of only four known survivors of the prison, was the first museum director. He is shown here with some of the metal shackles used to hold prisoners during interrogations.

CHAPTER FIVE

Recovering from the Wounds of Torture

Few victims of torture ever fully recover. Most are haunted by memories of their torments for the rest of their lives. Many suffer from a severe psychological condition known as post-traumatic stress disorder, or PTSD. Symptoms of PTSD include anxiety, flashbacks, insomnia, nightmares, memory lapses, depression, and suicide attempts. Torture victims often feel shame. Many are uncomfortable talking about their experiences, feeling humiliated by the abuses—often sexual—they were forced to endure. If they were forced to make confessions during their tortures—and if they implicated others who were then also tortured—they may feel a tremendous burden of guilt.

Many torture victims carry more than just mental anguish. Many bear scars or permanent and crippling injuries. Such physical trauma serves as a constant, daily reminder of the torture they endured. In a manual for physicians written by the Copenhagen-based Danish Institute against Torture, the organization lists no fewer than forty-one psychological

In 1994 Majur Malou, a Christian college student, was tortured in his home country of Sudan for speaking out against Sudan's Islamist government. He fled Sudan and in 1995 moved to San Diego, California. The San Diego–based Survivors of Torture International has helped him heal from his ordeal.

disorders as well as seventy-six physical maladies that torture victims typically suffer.

PTSD symptoms can be triggered almost anytime. The Danish institute's manual points out that a former torture victim can be traumatized by the simple act of entering a small room. States the manual, "Torture survivors frequently suffer from many causes of anxiety, elicited by objects that have previously been linked to their torture-related experiences . . . anxiety about darkness and in narrow rooms, based on having previously been imprisoned in darkness and narrow cells." Even hearing music that was played by their captors can spark symptoms of PTSD in torture survivors.

"THE SILENT VICTIMS OF TORTURE"

Somali lawyer Abukar Hassan Ahmed was campaigning for human rights in 1988 when he was arrested by his nation's military. At the time, the African nation was ruled by Mohamed

Siad Barre, one of the most ruthless dictators in the world. Siad Barre tolerated no dissent. After Ahmed's arrest, he was held in a tiny, windowless cell with no toilet. He was given little food. Over the course of several months, Ahmed was interrogated, sometimes for twenty-four hours at a time. His interrogators often beat and choked him. After nearly a year, Ahmed was released. He fled Somalia and settled in London. Since his release, Ahmed has suffered the crippling effects of his torture. The beatings damaged his spine, making it difficult for him to sit. The beatings also damaged Ahmed's bladder and left him permanently incontinent—unable to control his urine.

After Siad Barre's ouster in 1991, Ahmed felt safe enough to pursue his torturers, hoping to hold them legally accountable for their actions. With the aid of attorneys from the Center for Justice and Accountability, a San Francisco, California–based human rights organization, he was able to track down Abdi Aden Magan, the Somali colonel who oversaw his torture. The colonel had also fled Somalia and was living in Columbus, Ohio.

THE LONG ARM OF TORTURE

According to the International Rehabilitation Council for Torture Victims, victims of torture do not suffer in isolation. Says the organization, which is based in Copenhagen, Denmark, "Victims of torture do not suffer alone. Victims' families and friends are also greatly affected. Local society is damaged both through the trauma inflicted on its members but also through an instilled awareness that basic human rights are neither guaranteed nor respected. Freedom is not respected. People are not respected. The use of torture sends a strong warning to those within a political, social, or religious opposition, but also to normal citizens who cannot rightly claim to live in a free or safe society."

In 2013 attorneys for the Center for Justice and Accountability filed a federal lawsuit against him.

After the lawsuit was filed, Magan fled to Kenya. He never showed up for trial, and a federal judge ordered him to pay $15 million to Ahmed as compensation for the crippling effects of the torture. Ahmed doesn't think he will ever get the money from Magan because the former colonel's financial resources are limited. Still, Ahmed feels that torture victims should pursue cases against their former captors, if only to prove that nobody is above the law. Says Ahmed, "If you are black, you need justice. If you are white, you need justice. If you are yellow, you need justice. So everybody needs justice. It is universal. I don't seek only my justice, but I seek justice for other people also, because I call them the silent victims of torture—in Somalia or in other countries."

> "If you are black, you need justice. If you are white, you need justice. If you are yellow, you need justice. So everybody needs justice. It is universal."
> —Abukar Hassan Ahmed

HAUNTED BY THEIR ORDEALS

British citizen Peter Moore has largely recovered from the physical abuse he endured at the hands of his torturers. Nevertheless, Moore finds himself living with psychological scars that remain years after he was tortured by Iraqi militants.

In 2007 Moore found himself caught up in the turmoil of the Iraq War. He had been hired by the new US-backed leaders of Iraq to develop computer programs to help the government track its spending. Although not a combatant in Iraq's ongoing violence, Moore was still well aware of the dangers of the assignment. Since the fall of dictator Saddam Hussein in 2003,

Iraq had been besieged by terrorists, aiming to disrupt US-led efforts to democratize the nation. In many cases, citizens of the United States and its allies were the targets of their wrath.

Moore's company provided armed security guards to protect its employees. But on May 29, 2007, Moore and his bodyguards were attacked on a Baghdad street by an anti-American faction called Asaib Ahl al-Haq—the League of the Righteous. Four bodyguards were killed in the melee, and Moore was taken prisoner. As a captive, Moore was often tortured during his interrogations. He was beaten, humiliated, and subjected to psychological intimidation. On one occasion, he was forced to stand on a chair while his arms were strung from the ceiling. His captors kicked the chair away, and he was left to dangle in agony.

Perhaps the worst day of his captivity occurred when, shortly after his kidnapping, Moore was blindfolded, led outside, and shoved to the ground. He heard his captors talking, and since they spoke Arabic (he did not), he did not know what they were planning. Suddenly, a gun barrel was shoved against his head. Moore was certain that he was about to die.

And then he heard a click. No shot was fired. He heard laughter. It had been a cruel hoax.

For 947 days, Asaib Ahl al-Haq held Moore prisoner. They finally freed him in late 2009 after the British government agreed to release a prisoner captured by US forces in 2007. Years after his release, Moore says he is still haunted by memories of his captivity. "It feels strange," he says. "I feel like I've lost years that I have to catch up on. I've tried to get on with my life. But I have to say, it was an incomparable feeling to wake up in the morning and think, 'Is this going to be the last day that I live?' And to think that for every single morning for 2½ years?"

Dianna Ortiz, the nun abducted in Guatemala, is also haunted by the torture she endured. She writes, "After escaping from my torturers, I returned home to New Mexico, so traumatized that I recognized no one, not even my parents. I had virtually no memory of my life before my abduction; the only piece of my identity that remained was that I was a woman who was raped and forced to torture and murder another human being."

Ortiz filed a legal case against the Guatemalan security forces responsible for her torture and also pressured the US government to reveal thousands of pages of documents about human rights abuses in Guatemala. From these documents, she learned that the Guatemalan defense minister at the time of her torture had studied at the School of the Americas and that his security forces operated with US backing. Although the lawsuit against her torturers did not succeed, Ortiz went on to help other torture victims by founding the Torture Abolition and Survivor Support Coalition in Washington, DC. She also

Dianna Ortiz, who endured horrific torture during the "dirty wars" in Guatemala, brought a lawsuit against her tormentors but was unable to bring them to trial. She also founded an organization that helps other survivors of torture.

authored a book called *The Blindfold's Eyes: My Journey from Torture to Truth*, published in 2002.

STRENGTH IN THEIR SURVIVALS

In recent years, many psychologists have developed treatment plans for torture victims like Moore and Ortiz—encouraging them to talk about what they endured so they can better cope with their personal demons. Psychologists have found that many torture victims find strength in the fact that they managed to survive. Says University of Minnesota psychiatrist Joseph Westermeyer, "The goal of treatment is to help torture victims integrate the facts and feelings into their life history so they can let it go, say, 'It's part of my life, but there's lots of life left.'"

Mental health experts believe, though, that torture victims face obstacles in their treatments that other patients do not experience. Many torture victims do not trust other people because in captivity they did not know whom they could trust. During treatment, they may not completely trust their doctors and counselors. "Torture leaves such an indelible mark on its victims because, unlike victims of natural disasters, it's another human being inflicting the pain, and you're utterly helpless," says Eric Stover, formerly of the American Association for the Advancement of Science. "It destroys your trust in people."

During a victim's captivity, doctors and nurses may have been willing conspirators in torture, administering dangerous, disorienting drugs. As a result, torture victims may not trust the doctors with whom they work during post-torture recovery. They may be wary of medically prescribed antidepressant drugs and refuse to take them. Physicians and social workers are therefore specially trained to work closely with torture victims to develop trust.

LACKING SELF-SUFFICIENCY

After their release, few torture victims have the economic resources of Abukar Hassan Ahmed, who was able to leave Somalia and gain asylum in a safe country. For this reason, many torture victims continue to live in the countries where they were tortured. Many live in impoverished regions of the world, without access to health care, making it even harder to recover from the trauma of torture.

Suleiman Abdallah, for example, was arrested as a suspected terrorist in Somalia shortly after the September 2001 terrorist attacks. Abdallah protested his innocence, claiming that those who arrested him were trying to collect reward money offered by US intelligence agents. After his arrest, Abdallah was held at a detention center at a US Air Force base in Bagram, Afghanistan, where he was waterboarded and subjected to other tortures. During the waterboarding, interrogators would tell him, "We know you are a sea man, but here we have more water than out there in the sea. It never stops raining here."

Suleiman Abdallah was held at a detention center at a US Air Force base ... where he was waterboarded and subjected to other tortures.

For much of his incarceration, Abdallah was held in a wire-mesh cage. Finally and without explanation, he was released from custody in 2009. Instead of returning to Somalia, Abdallah made his way to Zanzibar, an island off the eastern coast of Africa that belongs to Tanzania. In Zanzibar he sought help from the group Physicians for Human Rights, which has attempted to provide him with medical care and psychological counseling.

But Zanzibar is poor. Hospitals and mental health

institutions there aren't equipped to meet the needs of the general population, let alone torture victims. Physicians for Human Rights has provided some help, including antidepressants. Also, a Kenyan psychologist travels to Zanzibar from time to time to counsel Abdallah. Sondra Crosby, a physician from Boston, Massachusetts, who has worked with Abdallah, says that he needs intensive counseling to overcome the trauma he experienced. She explains, "Suleiman's post-traumatic stress disorder left him unable to work and without means to support himself. His lack of self-sufficiency has led to further depression and feelings of inadequacy and shame, because he has to rely on his family for basic needs."

PROSECUTING THE TORTURERS

Some torture victims, such as Abukar Hassan Ahmed and Dianna Ortiz, attempt to bring legal cases against their torturers. And for many decades, international criminal tribunals have helped torture victims seek justice. Some courts have pursued criminal prosecutions against both torturers and political leaders who authorized the use of torture.

For example, one international court took action in the former southern European nation of Yugoslavia. In 1990, toward the end of the Cold War, the Communist-ruled nation broke up into individual states. A dictator, Slobodan Milosevic, emerged in the new state of Serbia. He waged a campaign of brutality and terror against the non-Serbian population of a region known as Kosovo. In 1998 and 1999, Milosevic's soldiers killed as many as thirteen thousand non-Serbian Kosovars and raped and tortured thousands more.

The brutality finally ended after the North Atlantic Treaty Organization (NATO)—an alliance of Western military powers—

THE INTERNATIONAL CRIMINAL COURT

The International Criminal Court (ICC), based in The Hague, is a permanent court set up in 2002 to prosecute war crimes and crimes against humanity. It was founded in response to the unwillingness or inability of some nations to bring torturers to trial. President George W. Bush chose not to have the United States join the ICC, and many members of the US Congress have been strongly opposed to US participation. Many feel that the United States—facing international criticism on a range of human rights issues—would be unfairly treated in the court. They prefer to see US citizens prosecuted under US law.

On the other hand, critics of the US position believe that Americans operating in international arenas must be exposed to international scrutiny. Says Mark J. McKeon, a US attorney who helped prosecute Slobodan Milosevic, "We cannot expect to regain our position of leadership in the world unless we hold ourselves to the same standards that we expect of others. That means punishing the most senior government officials responsible for these crimes. We have demanded this from other countries that have returned from walking on the dark side; we should expect no less from ourselves."

After Barack Obama was inaugurated as president in 2009, the United States began to work more closely with the court to prosecute international criminals. But the United States has not become an official member of the court.

bombed Serbian cities in the spring of 1999. Pressure from hundreds of thousands of protesters from across Serbia forced Milosevic to resign from power in October 2000. To win justice for Milosevic's victims, Serbia turned Milosevic over to the UN International Criminal Tribunal for the former Yugoslavia (ICTY) the next year to stand trial in The Hague, Netherlands.

As investigators sought evidence against Milosevic, they uncovered an interrogation center at a police station in Pristina, a city in Kosovo. Inside the building, they found cells as well as instruments of torture—clubs, machetes, wire garrotes for strangling prisoners, manacles for shackling prisoners to beds, and brass knuckles for punching victims. Some of the brass knuckles had been sharpened to slice into victims' flesh. After surveying the center, an investigator told reporters, "It's horrendous what people went through here—men and women. And there are children's clothes lying around here."

Milosevic's trial lasted four years. It ended without a verdict in 2006 when the defendant was found dead of a heart attack in his jail cell. Like the Milosevic trial, not all trials against torturers end with verdicts that satisfy victims. For example, in 2004—in the US-led War on Terror—the US Army Criminal Investigation Command charged a group of US Army interrogators with crimes related to torture and abuse of prisoners at the interrogation center at Bagram Airfield in Afghanistan. Two detainees had died in their cells, hanging by their shackled wrists. The victims had been deprived of sleep for days and had been beaten harshly in their legs. A medical examiner compared the injuries to those of someone who had been run over by a bus.

Of the fifteen army interrogators charged in the case, only six were sentenced to prison. The longest sentence served by any of these defendants was five months. The brother of one of the dead victims told a reporter, "My brother is dead. If they arrest 10,000 Americans, what good would that do me? I am angry with them, but this was the will of God. God is great, and God will punish them."

MONETARY COMPENSATION

In addition to carrying out criminal prosecutions, international courts also help torture victims seek monetary compensation for the abuses they endured. The European Court of Human Rights, established in the aftermath of World War II, has enabled torture victims to seek financial compensation from European nations that sanction torture. In 2012, for example, the court—meeting in the French city of Strasbourg—ordered the Russian government to pay convicted murderer Vitaly Buntov 45,000 euros (roughly $61,000) as compensation for torture he endured in a Russian jail in 2010. In its findings, the court made the following ruling:

> [Buntov] *alleged that soon after his transfer to the Plavsk* [penal] *colony he had learnt of the existence of an informal group of loyal convicts which helped the colony administration. That group (which the applicant called "the death squad") was composed solely of ethnic Russians. Their role was to threaten, beat or kill those convicts who opposed the colony administration, or those who had influential enemies outside the colony or refused to pay money to the administration. One of the cells in the colony (no. 112) was turned into a torture room and was used by the members of the group to "break down" those convicts who resisted the administration.*

Individual countries that have emerged from brutal dictatorships often attempt to compensate citizens who were tortured under their former regimes. For example, more than thirty years after the 1979 fall of the violent Khmer Rouge dictatorship in Cambodia, former torture victims are getting their day in court. The Cambodia Tribunal, organized by the United Nations and the government of Cambodia, has held trials against high-ranking members of the Khmer Rouge responsible for crimes against humanity and other charges dating to the 1970s.

During the dictatorship of Khmer Rouge leader Pol Pot (1975–1979), about two million Cambodians—25 percent of the population—were forced out of their homes and imprisoned. Hundreds of thousands were tortured and murdered. Survivor Bou Meng reports that he was accused of spying for the United States and repeatedly beaten in captivity. Bou's wife and four of his children were also arrested. All five died in Khmer Rouge prisons. "I lost five family members—my wife and four children—and some property under the Khmer Rouge," says Bou. "The court needs to calculate what this equals with money."

By 2014 the court had awarded reparations, or compensation, to thirteen victims of the Khmer Rouge. However, it is doubtful that those victims will be paid because the Cambodian government lacks the funds to do so. Private individuals, foundations, and international human rights organizations have stepped forward to donate $600,000 to a fund to help pay the reparations. The Cambodian government has made an appeal for additional donations to help pay reparations to Khmer Rouge victims.

CHAPTER SIX

Blowing the Whistle on Torture

In recent years, social media and the Internet have played important roles in exposing torture in some countries, particularly in the Middle East and North Africa. Dictators such as Hosni Mubarak of Egypt, Muammar Qaddafi of Libya, and Zine El-Abidine Ben Ali of Tunisia were ousted during the Arab Spring—a period of widespread public uprisings in Arab nations in 2010 and 2011.

Mubarak and the others had held firm control over the traditional press in their countries. So citizens of those countries could not count on journalists to expose torture and other wrongdoings by those in power. But those dictators could not stop people in their homes or Internet cafés from posting cell phone pictures of torture victims on social media sites. "Cell phones are now the essential tool of democracy in developing [poor] countries," says Hafez Abu Seada, the secretary-general of the Egyptian Organization for Human Rights.

Before he resigned in 2011 amid growing dissent and turmoil in his country, Mubarak had maintained dictatorial

During the Arab Spring uprisings of 2010 and 2011, people protested in the streets of Egypt and other nations in the Middle East and North Africa. In addition to demonstrating against repressive governments, citizens used the Internet to spread photographs of those who had been tortured in government custody.

power for thirty years, largely by turning his nation into a police state. During his rule, thousands of dissidents were tossed into jails, and many were tortured. By the first decade of the 2000s, though, the abuses committed by Mubarak's government—as well as similar abuses in nearby nations—were no longer secret. Information about the torture chambers of Egypt, Tunisia, Libya, and other countries was being revealed via the Internet.

Some of the first visual evidence of what was going on in Egypt surfaced in 2007, when blogger Wael Abbas posted videos of torture victim Mohamed Mamdouh Abdel-Aziz. The rail-thin thirteen-year-old boy's body was scarred with bruises and burn marks. The boy had been arrested in the town of Mansoura, about 75 miles (121 km) north of the Egyptian capital of Cairo, for the crime of stealing a few bags of tea. For that infraction of Egyptian law, Mohamed was arrested and tortured. The videos of Mohamed are believed to have been made by witnesses using cell phones just hours before the child died from his injuries.

The videos ignited international condemnation of Mubarak's regime and helped spark public dissent that would eventually succeed in ousting the dictator from power. "Activists that have worked to end torture have told me: 'You've done . . . in a few days what we were not able to do in 10 years,'" says Abbas.

ADVOCACY GROUPS

In the decades since the adoption of the Geneva Conventions, advocacy groups have formed to supplement the efforts of the United Nations and governments around the world to ensure respect for human rights. Groups such as Amnesty International and Human Rights Watch have grown into powerful influences in the campaign to end torture. Using funds from donations, these groups have waged their own investigations and have reported their findings.

In 2013, for example, New York City–based HRW issued a report on torture in the United Arab Emirates (UAE), providing as evidence handwritten letters obtained from prison inmates in the UAE. The report says,

> *Several detainees describe mistreatment that clearly meets the definition of torture as outlined in Article 1 of the United Nations Convention Against Torture and Other Cruel, Inhuman or Degrading Treatment or Punishment, which the UAE ratified in July 2012. "I*

was beaten with a plastic tube all over my body," one detainee said. *"I was tied to a chair and threatened with electrocution if I didn't talk. I was insulted and humiliated."*

The report quoted Joe Stork, deputy Middle East director at HRW. "The UAE's judicial system will lose all credibility if these allegations are swept under the carpet while the government's critics are put behind bars. Unless the government investigates and takes action, it will be hard to avoid concluding that torture is routine practice in the UAE."

Amnesty International, HRW, and other international organizations have no legal powers to act against abusive

By protesting publicly, people can bring attention to torture and other human rights abuses. Here, demonstrators in Kenya wear rainbow-flag masks to show support for gays and lesbians in nearby Uganda. In thirty-nine African nations, homosexuality is considered a crime. African gays and lesbians—especially some who have spoken out for gay rights—have been tortured and murdered.

regimes. Nevertheless, their findings are widely reported in the international media, and they help call attention to human rights abuses. In the early 1990s, for example, an Amnesty International report on torture and other human rights abuses in China helped convince the International Olympic Committee (IOC) to turn down China's bid to host the 2000 Summer Olympics. The Games were awarded instead to Sydney, Australia. The next year, the IOC voted to award the 2008 Summer Games to Beijing. During the next decade, China took steps to improve its human rights record and hosted the Games as planned.

> **An Amnesty International report on torture ... in China helped convince the International Olympic Committee ... to turn down China's bid to host the 2000 Summer Olympics.**

In recent years, China has become a powerful force in the world economy. Chinese leaders realize that Western democracies are hesitant to enter into trade agreements with a country that maintains a poor human rights record, so China has taken initial steps to outlaw torture and other human rights abuses. For example, in 2013 the Supreme People's Court—the highest court in China—issued a directive banning the use of torture to produce confessions from suspected criminals.

But human rights groups are skeptical about the ban and predict that torture and other human rights abuses will continue in China. A reporter with HRW explains, "The Supreme People's Court's announcement should not pass as a real reform yet. For one, it only speaks to the courts, while it's the police, a much more powerful institution than China's weak courts, that does the torturing. . . . The Supreme Court's move is an encouraging step. It demonstrates at the very least that there are people inside the system pushing for progress, and that alone is significant. At the same time, let's not be naive about the improvements one paper document can bring to the system."

FIGHTING TORTURE IN AFRICA

Charted by the African Union (an alliance of African states), the African Commission on Human and Peoples' Rights (ACHPR) is dedicated to fighting torture and other abuses across the African continent. Africa has a poor human rights record—thirty-seven of fifty-four African Union states have no legislation criminalizing torture. ACHPR is working to change this. It sponsors seminars, conferences, and other educational programs in support of human rights. It investigates allegations of torture and rules on torture cases.

In a recent ruling, ACHPR found the government of Zimbabwe responsible for the torture of human rights lawyer Gabriel Shumba. While meeting with clients in 2003, Shumba was arrested by Zimbabwean police and intelligence officers. During his detention, interrogators kicked him, beat him, burned him with chemicals, and subjected him to electric shocks. He was forced to sign a confession stating that he was conspiring to overthrow the government of Zimbabwean dictator Robert Mugabe. After his release, Shumba fled to South Africa. He knew that if he returned to Zimbabwe to seek justice, he would probably be rearrested. So he took his case to the ACHPR. The commission ruled in March 2013 that Zimbabwe had violated Article 5 of the African Charter on Human and Peoples' Rights, which prohibits torture, and ordered Zimbabwe to pay monetary compensation to Shumba.

The ruling was seen as an important step in the fight against human rights abuses in Zimbabwe and other African nations. Says David Padilla, Shumba's lawyer, "This decision is emblematic of the widespread use of state terror to coerce and cow a subject population. It is not merely a legal decision in favour of a single victim but rather a recognition by Africa's most important and prestigious institution that the practice of disappearing people and beating them to within an inch of their lives will no longer be ignored by Zimbabwe's neighbours."

THE WHISTLE-BLOWERS

Whistle-blowers, individuals or organizations that go public with confidential government documents or other insider information, are another piece of the puzzle. The whistle-blowing website WikiLeaks has exposed several cases of torture by leaking secret US Army documents to media sources. In 2010, for example, WikiLeaks released US military documents indicating that during the Iraq War, US-trained Iraqi troops tortured suspected terrorists, subjecting some to electrical shocks while using power drills to inflict injuries on others. Moreover, the documents revealed that the incidents of torture were brought to the attention of US military officers, who took no action to stop them.

In many cases, potential whistle-blowers struggle with inner turmoil: Should they follow orders and keep quiet about what they know of abusive practices, or should they tell what they know because torture is morally repugnant to them? John Kiriakou is one such individual. He joined the CIA in 1990 as an analyst. He later became a CIA agent. His job was to recruit foreign informants and to oversee covert operations in trouble spots around the world. In 2002 Kiriakou flew to Pakistan to

TORTURE...AT COLLEGE?

In 2013 Justin Stuart, aged nineteen, was stripped to his underwear and forced to stand waist-deep in a trash can filled with ice. His tormenters sprayed him with a garden hose and dumped icy water on his head. Over subsequent weeks, Stuart and other young people were beaten repeatedly with paddles and forced to drink large quantities of alcohol until they passed out. They were also humiliated—forced to dress in women's clothing and in diapers. Sometimes they were locked in dark basements overnight without food, water, or access to toilets. "It honestly reminded me of Guantanamo Bay," Stuart says.

Had Stuart been captured by foreign terrorists? No, he had undergone a hazing ritual as part of the process of joining Sigma Alpha Epsilon (SAE) fraternity at Salisbury University in Maryland. As part of the ritual, recruits were forced to undergo weeks of abuse that university administrators decided was akin to torture. Following the reports of hazing at SAE in 2013, the university temporarily suspended its chapter of the fraternity.

take custody of al-Qaeda leader Abu Zubaydah, a planner of the September 2001 terrorist attacks. Zubaydah had been wounded in a shootout with Pakistani police and was then turned over to the US military. Kiriakou learned that after Zubaydah had been taken into US custody, he had been waterboarded.

That same year, a supervisor asked Kiriakou to undergo training in the enhanced interrogation techniques the CIA was using on captured al-Qaeda terrorists, among them waterboarding and prolonged sleep deprivation. Kiriakou wrestled with his conscience; he spoke with a senior CIA official about the morality of torture; and ultimately declined to participate, believing the techniques crossed the line of acceptable interrogation methods. Two years later, in 2004, Kiriakou resigned from the CIA after arguing with his supervisor over a poor performance evaluation. When he

In 2007 former CIA agent John Kiriakou spoke on television about the torture of al-Qaeda prisoners by US forces in Pakistan. The information was supposed to be kept secret. For revealing it, Kiriakou was sentenced to thirty months in prison.

resigned, Kiriakou signed nondisclosure agreements—promising never to reveal information about his CIA service.

After leaving the CIA, Kiriakou found himself in demand as a technical consultant to Hollywood production companies making movies about the wars in Iraq and Afghanistan. By 2007 he was well known in news and entertainment circles for his expertise in intelligence and was often interviewed on television news programs. By this time, rumors had surfaced that CIA agents and military personnel were using waterboarding and other enhanced interrogation techniques on captured prisoners in Iraq and Afghanistan. During an interview on ABC News in 2007, reporter Brian Ross asked Kiriakou whether the rumors about waterboarding were true. Kiriakou confirmed the rumors. He also told Ross that the CIA had waterboarded Zubaydah and had managed to break the terrorist's will after just thirty-five seconds. He said, "The next day, [Zubaydah] told his interrogator that Allah [God] had visited him in his cell during the night and told him to cooperate. . . . From that day on, he answered every question. The . . . information he provided disrupted a number of attacks, maybe dozens of attacks."

Although Kiriakou had not participated in the waterboarding of Zubaydah, he had knowingly broken his nondisclosure agreements by going public with what he knew. Kiriakou's revelations about waterboarding cost him his freedom. In 2012 he pleaded guilty to the federal crime of disclosing classified (secret) information. He was sentenced

To show the horrors of waterboarding, a group called World Can't Wait simulated the practice at a protest in New York City in 2009. The protesters urged prosecution of American leaders who had approved waterboarding of terror suspects.

to thirty months in prison. In early 2013, he began serving his sentence in a federal prison near Pittsburgh, Pennsylvania.

Kiriakou knew full well that when he revealed all he knew about waterboarding, he was breaking the law and would likely face legal consequences. Yet his conscience would not permit him to remain silent about an interrogation technique he knew to be nothing less than torture. He says, "Even if torture works, it cannot be tolerated—not in one case or a thousand or a million."

"OUR BEST SHOT"

In the twenty-first century, torture is still very much a fact of life around the world. While human rights activists and others have made progress in exposing torture and in ousting regimes that abuse their citizens through torture, the practice may never completely disappear.

Scholar Darius Rejali explains that torture is possible whenever one person has absolute power over another. He says, "There's not a single country or a single privileged group that doesn't [make] its contribution to torture. . . . Nobody is morally pure." He also notes that "anyone who has any exposure to policing or military life knows that social conditions [can] drive ordinary people to violence." Torturers take the easy way out, he explains. "Why do the hard work of intelligent policing when you have a bat? Why develop the human intelligence to penetrate al Qaeda with a mole [spy] when you can arrest a person and stick his head under water? This behavior happens only when people allow it, and it also destroys real policing skill."

> **"Even if torture works, it cannot be tolerated—not in one case or a thousand or a million."**
> —former CIA agent John Kiriakou

Despite humankind's long and terrible history of torture, Rejali is optimistic that we can prevent it. He says:

> *Human rights monitoring really does work and affects the behavior of torturers. Some people may think that their check to their Amnesty International group or church group or local cop watch doesn't work, but actually historical evidence is clear that these groups have an effect. If these groups work with people on the inside* [of government and the military] *that have an equal commitment to reform, they can produce a world without torture, and that's our best shot.*

CRITICAL ANALYSIS

Soon after the September 11, 2001, al-Qaeda terrorist attacks on the United States, US and NATO troops invaded Afghanistan to oust that nation's leadership, which harbored key operatives of the terrorist group. In 2003 the United States also attacked Iraq, charging that Iraqi dictator Saddam Hussein was stockpiling weapons of mass destruction. As prisoners were captured in Iraq and Afghanistan, officials in the administration of US president George W. Bush examined whether enhanced interrogation violated the Geneva Conventions against torture and whether such techniques were justified. The following quotes lay out some of the arguments:

The Geneva Conventions state that "no physical or mental torture, nor any other form of coercion, may be inflicted on prisoners of war to secure from them information of any kind whatever. Prisoners of war who refuse to answer may not be threatened, insulted, or exposed to unpleasant or disadvantageous treatment of any kind."

US attorney general Alberto Gonzalez argued in 2002 that the Geneva Conventions did not apply to terrorist groups. He said, "The war against terrorism is a new kind of war. It is not the traditional clash between nations adhering to the laws of war that formed the backdrop for the [Geneva Conventions]. The nature of the new war places a high premium on other factors, such as the ability to quickly obtain information from captured terrorists and their sponsors in order to avoid further atrocities against American citizens, and the need to try terrorists for war crimes such as wantonly killing civilians."

US secretary of state Colin Powell countered in 2002 that "[not following the Geneva Conventions] will undermine the protections of the law of war for our troops, both in this specific conflict and in general. . . . It will undermine public support among critical allies, making military cooperation more difficult to sustain."

Deputy Assistant Attorney General John Yoo argued in 2003 that "depending upon the precise factual circumstances, such [enhanced interrogation] techniques may be necessary to ensure the protection of the government's interest here—national security."

President George W. Bush told reporters in 2004, "Look, let me make very clear the position of my government and our country. We do not condone torture. I have never ordered torture. I will never order torture. The values of this country are such that torture is not a part of our soul and our being."

Attorneys for the American Civil Liberties Union and the Open Justice Initiative assessed George Bush's record on torture in 2007. They said, "The Bush administration has professed a commitment to democracy and human rights and claimed solidarity with those who struggle against tyranny. But the documents show unambiguously that the administration has adopted some of the methods of the most tyrannical regimes. Documents from Guantanamo describe prisoners shackled in excruciating 'stress positions,' held in freezing-cold cells, forcibly stripped, hooded, terrorized with military dogs, and deprived of human contact for months. Documents from Afghanistan and Iraq describe prisoners beaten, kicked, electrocuted, and burned."

Working alone or in a group, consider each of these statements. Based on what you've read in this book and on additional online research, which arguments seem most valid? Write a persuasive essay explaining why you agree or disagree with each statement. Craft solid arguments and include direct quotes from experts and other government officials to support your position.

GLOSSARY

asylum: protection provided by a nation to someone fleeing another nation for fear of arrest, punishment, or persecution

Cold War: a period of political, economic, and military hostility between the United States and the Communist Soviet Union, lasting from 1946 to 1991. During the Cold War, the United States worked to prevent the spread of Communism around the world without engaging in direct warfare.

Communism: an economic system in which the government controls all business activity, with no private enterprise or private property ownership

coup: the violent overthrow of an existing government, usually by a small group

detainee: someone held in custody for political or military reasons

dissent: political opposition to a government and its policies

Enlightenment: a period in European history in the eighteenth century when philosophers and other thinkers emphasized the use of reason and evidence over tradition and faith

Geneva Conventions: a series of international agreements initiated after World War II that provide for the humane treatment of civilians, prisoners, and wounded people during wartime

genocide: the deliberate, systematic, and widespread killing of members of a racial, political, or ethnic group

Gulag: a system of prison labor camps in remote regions of the former Soviet Union, established under dictator Joseph Stalin in the 1930s. Treatment in the camps, which were closed in the 1950s, was harsh and typically involved torture.

heretic: a person who does not follow established religious teachings

Inquisition: an effort by the Roman Catholic Church, through a network of interrogators, courts, and judges, to root out and punish nonbelievers and other dissidents. The Inquisition took place in many European countries and their colonies from the 1200s to the mid-1800s. Inquisitors relied on forms of torture to extract confessions and information from suspects.

insurgent: a rebel or revolutionary, who revolts against an established government

intelligence: information concerning an enemy or suspected enemy

interrogate: to question formally and systematically

police state: a nation that uses a police force, with no legal restraints on how it proceeds, to maintain order, spy on citizens, and punish citizens. Such states often rely on torture to instill fear and to limit dissent.

reparation: payment to compensate for a wrongdoing such as torture

resistance: an underground organization in a conquered or occupied country that carries out sabotage and secret operations against the conquering or occupying forces

revolutionary: a person who fights for a fundamental change in a nation's government

subversive: a person who tries to overthrow or undermine a government by working secretly from within government institutions

terrorism: the use or threat of violence to create fear and alarm, usually to promote a movement or cause

torture: the intentional infliction of severe pain or suffering, either physical or mental, by a public official or by someone acting in an official capacity, done to obtain information or a confession from someone, to punish someone, or to intimidate or coerce someone

TIMELINE

300s BCE   Greek philosopher Aristotle endorses torture as an effective way of forcing accused criminals to tell the truth.

71 BCE   Roman soldiers crucify six thousand followers of Spartacus, leader of a rebellion against the Roman Republic.

ca. 1100 CE   The epic poem *La Chanson de Roland (The Song of Roland)* describes a military campaign of Frankish emperor Charlemagne, with descriptions of torture inflicted on the emperor's enemies.

1100s–1800s   During a period called the Inquisition, the Roman Catholic Church uses torture to extract confessions from heretics. Targets include Protestants, Muslims, Jews, and others who defy social norms.

1307–1323   French inquisitor Bernard Gui uses torture to extract confessions from more than six hundred suspected heretics.

circa 1310s   Italian poet Dante Alighieri describes imaginary tortures inflicted in hell in *Inferno*, a section of his epic poem *The Divine Comedy*.

1600s–1865   Slavery prevails in the American South. Many slave owners use whipping and other tortures to punish slaves for perceived wrongdoings.

1764   Italian jurist Cesare Beccaria publishes *Of Crimes and Punishments*, which contains his ideas about criminal justice. In one chapter, he outlines arguments against the use of torture.

1789   Leaders of the French Revolution, inspired by the American war for independence from Great Britain, publish the *Declaration of the Rights of Man and of the Citizen*. The document promotes ideals of democracy and human rights.

1791   US leaders ratify the first ten amendments to the US Constitution, known as the Bill of Rights. The amendments list the fundamental rights and freedoms of citizens.

The Eighth Amendment prohibits cruel and unusual punishment.

1798 French general Napoleon Bonaparte denounces torture in a letter to a French government official.

1863 Swiss businessman Henri Dunant organizes the First Geneva Conference. Conference attendees establish rules for the humane conduct of war. These rules become known as the First Geneva Convention.

1865 The US Congress ratifies the Thirteenth Amendment to the US Constitution, outlawing slavery.

1919 Victorious nations of World War I form the League of Nations, an association that works to resolve international disputes. Although the idea for the league comes from US president Woodrow Wilson, the United States never officially joins the league, which dissolves in 1946.

1930s–1950s Millions of criminals and political prisoners are locked up in the Gulag, a system of prison camps in the Soviet Union. Inmates there perform hard labor and sometimes undergo tortures such as exposure to extreme cold, sleep deprivation, and starvation.

1939–1945 Doctors working for the Nazi government in Germany perform torturous medical experiments on inmates at concentration camps. Victims are exposed to extreme cold, are injected with chemical poisons, undergo surgeries without anesthesia, and are subjected to many other forms of torture. The Nazi secret police forces also torture enemies of the Nazi regime.

1945 Representatives from fifty nations meet in San Francisco, California, to draw up a charter for the United Nations, an international peacekeeping organization.

1946 The United States establishes the School of the Americas in Panama. There, instructors from the Central Intelligence Agency and the US military teach torture techniques to military and police personnel from Latin America.

1948 The United Nations adopts the Universal Declaration of Human Rights, which prohibits torture.

1970–1990s Governments in Chile, Argentina, El Salvador, Nicaragua, and Guatemala wage "dirty wars" against their own citizens. Military and police forces, many of them trained at the School of the Americas, victimize suspected enemies of the state, including human rights activists, political protesters, artists, and intellectuals. Many are held without charges, tortured, and murdered.

1975–1979 In Cambodia, the Khmer Rouge government imprisons, tortures, and murders millions of citizens.

1984 The United Nations passes the Convention against Torture and Other Cruel, Inhuman and Degrading Treatment or Punishment.

1996 Journalists and the US public learn about the School of the Americas torture manuals. Protesters call for the school to be shut down.

1998–1999 In Serbia, dictator Slobodan Milosevic oversees the torture and murder of thousands of the region's non-Serbian population.

2001 Members of the Islamist terror group al-Qaeda hijack four US airliners and crash three of them into buildings in New York and Virginia on September 11. The fourth plane crashes in a field in Pennsylvania. Some Americans endorse torture techniques to root out further terrorist plots.

2002 US attorney general Alberto Gonzalez argues that the Geneva Conventions do not apply to terrorist groups. Nations around the world set up the International Criminal Court to prosecute war crimes, crimes against humanity, genocide, and other atrocities. Preferring to see its citizens tried in US courts, the United States chooses not to join the court.

2003 In an effort to extract intelligence, US interrogators use waterboarding 183 times on Khalid Sheikh Mohammed, a planner of the September 11 attacks. A group of US Army interrogators torture suspected terrorists at Bagram Airfield in Afghanistan.

2004 Photos leaked to the press show torture of Iraqi detainees at the Abu Ghraib military prison in Iraq. A full investigation reveals extensive torture by US military guards at the prison.

2005 Suspected terrorists held by the US military at Guatanamo Bay in Cuba begin a series of hunger strikes to protest what they see as their unlawful detainment. Guards keep them alive by force-feeding, a process that many describe as torture.

2006 A court organized by Cambodia and the United Nations begins to try former Khmer Rouge leaders for war crimes, genocide, and crimes against humanity, including torture, committed between 1975 and 1979.

2007 Former CIA agent John Kiriakou speaks on US television about the waterboarding of al-Qaeda prisoners in Pakistan. He is later sentenced to thirty months in prison for revealing the confidential information.

2010 The whistle-blowing website WikiLeaks releases military documents detailing the torture of terrorist suspects by US-trained troops in Iraq.

2013 The Supreme People's Court of China bans the use of torture to extract confessions from suspected criminals.

2014 Thousands of photographs smuggled out of Syria reveal that Syrian forces, under the leadership of President Bashar al-Assad, have routinely used torture, including beatings, electrocution, strangulation, and starvation against those fighting to overthrow the Assad regime.

SOURCE NOTES

6   "Kazakhstan: No Accountability for Entrenched Torture," Amnesty International, July 11, 2013, http://www.amnesty.org/en/news/kazakhstan -no-accountability-entrenched-torture-2013-07-11.

6   "Roza Is a Leader: That's Why They Jailed Her," *libcom.org*, December 7, 2013, http://www.libcom.org/news/roza-leader-thats-why-they-jailed-her-07122013.

7   Henry Shue, "Torture," in *Torture: A Collection*, ed. Sanford Levinson (Oxford: Oxford University Press, 2004), 47.

11   Mark P. Donnelly and Daniel Diehl, *The Big Book of Pain: Torture and Punishment through History* (Gloucestershire, UK: History Press, 2008), 37.

11   Will Durant, *Caesar and Christ: The Story of Civilization III* (New York: Simon and Schuster, 1944), 138.

13   *The Song of Roland*, trans. Dorothy L. Sayers (Middlesex, UK: Penguin, 1971), 121.

15   *The Comedy of Dante Alighieri*, trans. Dorothy L. Sayers (Middlesex, UK: Penguin, 1973), 215.

15   Ibid.

16–17   Will Durant, *The Age of Faith: The Story of Civilization IV* (New York: Simon and Schuster, 1950), 781–782.

18   Murray N. Rothbard, "The Brutality of Slavery," *Ludwig von Mises Institute*, January 28, 2013, http://mises.org/daily/6347/.

18–19   Milton Meltzer, *Slavery: A World History*, vol. 2 (Cambridge, MA: Da Capo Press, 1993), 164.

20   Richard Bernstein, "Torture Recounted at Barbie Trial," *New York Times*, May 23, 1987, 3.

21–22   Ibid.

23–24   Aleksandr I. Solzhenitsyn, *The Gulag Archipelago* (New York: Harper & Row, 1974), 113–114.

26   John McCain, *Faith of My Fathers*, with Mark Salter (New York: Random House, 1999), 224.

27   Michael Winship, "The Torturing Company We Keep," *Consortium News*, July 25, 2008, http://www.consortiumnews.com/2008/072508a.html.

27–28   Ross Johnston, "Torture, Executions Are Daily Occurrences at North Korea's 'Rehabilitation' Gulags," *National Post* (Toronto), February 3, 2012, http://news .nationalpost.com/2012/02/03/torture-executions-are-daily-occurrences-at-north -koreas-rehabilitation-gulags.

28–29   "Confessions of a Zimbabwe Torturer," *BBC*, July 6, 2007, http://news.bbc .co.uk/2/hi/africa/6275152.stm.

30   "Cameroon: LGBTI Rights Activist Found Dead, Tortured," Human Rights Watch, July 16, 2013, http://www.hrw.org/news/2013/07/16/cameroon-lgbti -rights-activist-found-dead-tortured.

31   Paul Kelso, "Saudi Bomb Victim's Torture Ordeal—and Britain's Silence," *Guardian* (London), January 31, 2002, http://www.theguardian.com /world/2002/jan/31/saudiarabia.politics.

31   Darius Rejali, *Torture and Democracy* (Princeton, NJ: Princeton University Press, 2007), 208.

33   "Terrorist Video Shows American Pleading," *CNN*, December 26, 2013, http:// transcripts.cnn.com/TRANSCRIPTS/1312/26/cnr.09.html.

33 Ibid.

34 Joey, *Hit No. 29*, with Dave Fisher (New York: Pocket Books, 1975), 19.

36 Anne Marie O'Connor and William Booth, "Torture Surges in Mexico's Drug War, Rights Group Says," *Washington Post*, November 9, 2011, http://www.washingtonpost.com/world/americas/torture-surges-in-mexicos-drug-war-rights-group-says/2011/11/09/gIQAphSI6M_story.html.

38 Ian Fisher, "Iraqi Recounts Hours of Abuse by US Troops," *New York Times*, May 5, 2004.

39 Neil MacFarquhar, "Revulsion at Prison Abuse Provokes Scorn for the US," *New York Times*, May 5, 2004.

40 "Syria Crisis: 'Torture' Photos Shown to UN Security Council," *BBC News Middle East*, April 15, 2014, http://www.bbc.com/news/world-middle-east-27044203.

41–42 Cesare Beccaria, *On Crimes and Punishments and Other Writings* (Cambridge: Cambridge University Press, 1995), 39.

42 "Of Crimes and Punishments, Cesare Beccaria, 'Of Torture,'" *Constitution.org*, accessed March 24, 2014, http://www.constitution.org/cb/crim_pun16.htm.

42 Jay Luvaas, *Napoleon on the Art of War* (New York: Free Press, 1999), 11.

46 "Convention for the Amelioration of the Condition of the Wounded in Armies in the Field. Geneva, 22 August 1864," International Committee of the Red Cross, 2014, accessed April 17, 2014, http://www.icrc.org/ihl/52d68d14de6160e0c1256 3da005fdb1b/87a3bb58c1c44f0dc125641a005a06e0.

48 "Convention against Torture and Other Cruel, Inhuman or Degrading Treatment or Punishment," University of Minnesota Human Rights Library, December 24, 2013, http://www1.umn.edu/humanrts/instree/h2catoc.htm.

49 "Convention against Torture and Other Cruel, Inhuman or Degrading Treatment or Punishment," United Nations High Commissioner for Human Rights, 2012, accessed April 17, 2014, http://www.ohchr.org/EN/ProfessionalInterest/Pages/CAT.aspx.

52 Willard C. Matthias, *America's Strategic Blunders: Intelligence Analysis and National Security Policy, 1936–1991* (University Park: Pennsylvania State University Press, 2001), 11.

53–54 "The CIA's Textbook on Torture," *St. Louis Post-Dispatch*, February 7, 1997, C-10.

54 Walter Pincus, "CIA Manual Discussed 'Coercive' Interrogation; Latin Countries Used 1983 Training Book," *Washington Post*, January 28, 1997, A-9.

55 Frederick Henry Gareau, *State Terrorism and the United States: From Counterinsurgency to the War on Terrorism* (London: Zed Books, 2004), 25.

57 State University of New York, "Close School of Americas; Release Jailed Protestors," September 27, 1996, http://www.hartford-hwp.com/archives/40/025.html.

57 Suzy Hansen, "Why Terrorism Works," *Salon.com*, September 12, 2002, http://www.salon.com/2002/09/12/dershowitz_3.

59 Ibid.

60 *What Went Wrong: Torture and the Office of Legal Counsel in the Bush Administration: Hearing Before the Subcommittee of Administrative Oversight and the Courts of the Committee on the Judiciary United States Senate*, 111th Cong. (May 13, 2009) (statement of Ali Soufan), http://www.judiciary.senate.gov/hearings/testimony.cfm?id=e655f9e2809e5476862f735da14945e6&wit_id=e655f9e2809e5476862f735da14945e6-1-2.

60   Ibid.

60–61   Ibid.

61   Ibid.

61   Ibid.

61   Hansen, "Why Terrorism Works."

62   Charles Krauthammer, "The Truth about Torture," *Weekly Standard*, December 2, 2005, http://www.weeklystandard.com/Content/Public/Articles/000/000/006/400rhqav.asp?page=1.

62   Sam Harris, "In Defense of Torture," *Huffington Post*, October 17, 2005, http://www.huffingtonpost.com/sam-harris/in-defense-of-torture_b_8993.html.

63   Eric Margolis, "America's Shame," *LewRockwell.com*, accessed April 28, 2009, http://archive.lewrockwell.com/margolis/margolis145.html.

63   Robin Lindley, "Torture in Democratic Societies: Interview with Darius Rejali," *George Mason University's History News Network*. 2014, http://hnn.us/article/51419, accessed May 22, 2014.

64   Charlie Savage, "Election to Decide Future Interrogation Methods in Terrorism Cases," *New York Times*, September 28, 2012.

68   Bengt H. Sjölund, ed., *RCT Field Manual on Rehabilitation* (Copenhagen: Rehabilitation and Research Centre for Torture Victims, 2007), 16.

69   "Defining Torture," International Rehabilitation Council for Torture Victims, 2013, accessed March 24, 2014, http://www.irct.org/what-is-torture/defining-torture.aspx.

70   Kathy Lynn Gray, "$15 Million Awarded to Somali Torture Victim," *Columbus Dispatch*, August 21, 2013, http://www.dispatch.com/content/stories/public/2013/08/20/human-rights-judgment.html.

70   Ibid.

71   Hampton Sides, "Hostage," *Men's Health*, December 2011, 6.

72   Dianna Ortiz, "Dianna Ortiz," Robert F. Kennedy Center for Justice and Human Rights, 2014, accessed April 17, 2014, http://rfkcenter.org/dianna-ortiz-7.

73   Daniel Goleman, "Grim Specialty Emerges as Therapists Treat Victims of Torture," *New York Times*, April 25, 1989, http://www.nytimes.com/1989/04/25/science/grim-specialty-emerges-as-therapists-treat-victims-of-torture.html?pagewanted=all&src=pm.

73   Ibid.

74   Clara Gutteridge, "Is There Freedom after Torture?," *Nation*, July 16–23, 2012, 22.

75   Ibid., 23.

76   Mark J. McKeon, "Why We Must Prosecute," *Washington Post*, April 28, 2009, http://www.washingtonpost.com/wp-dyn/content/article/2009/04/27/AR2009042702693.html.

77   Julian Borger, "Bloody Paper Chain May Link Torture to Milosevic," *Guardian* (London), June 17, 1999, http://www.theguardian.com/world/1999/jun/18/balkans3.

77   Tim Golden, "Years after 2 Afghans Died, Abuse Case Falters," *New York Times*, February 13, 2006.

78 *Case of Buntov v. Russia*, European Court of Human Rights, June 5, 2012, http://hudoc.echr.coe.int/sites/eng/pages/search.aspx?i=001-111176#{"item id":["001-111176"]}.

79 Stephen Kurczy, "For Former Khmer Rouge Prisoners, Reparations Are Key to Justice," *Christian Science Monitor*, July 3, 2009, 1.

80 Steven Stanek, "Egyptian Bloggers Expose Horrors of Police Torture," *San Francisco Chronicle*, October 9, 2007, http://www.sfgate.com/politics/article /Egyptian-bloggers-expose-horror-of-police-torture-2536284.php.

82 Ibid.

82–83 "UAE: Reports of Systematic Torture in Jails," Human Rights Watch, June 27, 2013, http://www.hrw.org/news/2013/06/27/uae-reports-systematic-torture-jails.

83 Ibid.

84–85 Nicholas Bequelin, "Dispatches: China Bans Confessions Obtained under Torture (Again)," Human Rights Watch, November 21, 2013, http://www.hrw.org/news /2013/11/21/dispatches-china-bans-confessions-obtained-under-torture again.

86 "African Commission Finds Zimbabwe Responsible for Torture of a Human Rights Lawyer," Movement for Democratic Change, March 22, 2013, http:// mdctsa.wordpress.com/tag/gabriel-shumba/.

87 John Hechninger and David Glovin, "Deadliest Frat's Icy 'Torture' of Pledges Evokes Tarantino Films," *Bloomberg News*, December 30, 2013, http://www .bloomberg.com/news/2013-12-30/deadliest-frat-s-icy-torture-of-pledges-evokes -tarantino-films.html.

89 Richard Esposito and Brian Ross, "Coming in from the Cold: CIA Spy Calls Waterboarding Necessary but Torture," *ABC News*, December 10, 2007, http:// abcnews.go.com/Blotter/story?id=3978231.

90 Steve Coll, "The Spy Who Said Too Much," *New Yorker*, April 1, 2013, 60.

90 Robin Lindley, "Torture in Democratic Societies: Interview with Darius Rejali," *George Mason University History's New Network*, 2014, accessed April 17, 2014, http://hnn.us/article/51419.

91 Ibid.

92 "Convention (III) Relative to the Treatment of Prisoners of War. Geneva, 12 August 1949," International Committee of the Red Cross, May 14, 2012, http:// www.icrc.org/ihl.nsf/7c4d08d9b287a42141256739003e636b/6fef854a3517b75ac 125641e004a9e68.

92 Neil A. Lewis, "A Guide to the Memos on Torture," *New York Times*, 2005, accessed March 24, 2014, http://www.nytimes.com/ref/international/24MEMO -GUIDE.html?_r=0.

92–93 Ibid.

93 "Memo Regarding the Torture and Military Interrogation of Alien Unlawful Combatants Held Outside the United States," American Civil Liberties Union, March 14, 2003, https://www.aclu.org/national-security/memo-regarding -torture-and-military-interrogation-alien-unlawful-combatants-held-o.

93 "Bush: 'I Have Never Ordered Torture,'" CNN, June 22, 2004, http://www.cnn .com/2004/ALLPOLITICS/06/22/rumsfeld.memo.

93 Jameel Jaffer and Amrit Singh, *Administration of Torture* (New York: Columbia University, 2007, 2.

SELECTED BIBLIOGRAPHY

Bernstein, Richard. "Torture Recounted at Barbie Trial." *New York Times*, May 23, 1987.

Borger, Julian. "Bloody Paper Chain May Link Torture to Milosevic." *Guardian* (London), June 17, 1999. http://www.theguardian.com/world/1999/jun/18/balkans3.

"Cameroon: LGBTI Rights Activist Found Dead, Tortured." Human Rights Watch, July 16, 2013. http://www.hrw.org/news/2013/07/16/cameroon-lgbti-rights-activist-found -dead-tortured.

"Close School of Americas; Release Jailed Protestors." State University of New York, September 27, 1996. http://www.hartford-hwp.com/archives/40/025.html.

"Confessions of a Zimbabwe Torturer." *BBC*, July 6, 2007. http://news.bbc.co.uk/2/hi /africa/6275152.stm.

Donnelly, Mark P., and Daniel Diehl. *The Big Book of Pain: Torture and Punishment through History*. Gloucestershire, UK: History Press, 2008.

Durant, Will. *The Age of Faith: The Story of Civilization IV*. New York: Simon and Schuster, 1950.

———. *Caesar and Christ: The Story of Civilization III*. New York: Simon and Schuster, 1944.

Esposito, Richard, and Brian Ross. "Coming in from the Cold: CIA Spy Calls Waterboarding Necessary but Torture." *ABC News*, December 10, 2007. http://abcnews .go.com/Blotter/story?id=3978231.

Gareau, Frederick Henry. *State Terrorism and the United States: From Counterinsurgency to the War on Terrorism*. London: Zed Books, 2004.

Golden, Tim. "Years after 2 Afghans Died, Abuse Case Falters." *New York Times*, February 13, 2006.

Goleman, Daniel. "Grim Specialty Emerges as Therapists Treat Victims of Torture." *New York Times*, April 25, 1989. http://www.nytimes.com/1989/04/25/science/grim-specialty -emerges-as-therapists-treat-victims-of-torture.html?pagewanted=all&src=pm.

Gray, Kathy Lynn. "$15 Million Awarded to Somali Torture Victim." *Columbus Dispatch*, August 21, 2013. http://www.dispatch.com/content/stories/public/2013/08/20/human -rights-judgment.html.

Hansen, Suzy. "Why Terrorism Works." *Salon.com*, September 12, 2002. http://www .salon.com/2002/09/12/dershowitz_3.

Hechninger, John, and David Glovin. "Deadliest Frat's Icy 'Torture' of Pledges Evokes Tarantino Films." *Bloomberg News*, December 30, 2013. http://www.bloomberg.com /news/2013-12-30/deadliest-frat-s-icy-torture-of-pledges-evokes-tarantino-films.html.

Johnston, Ross. "Torture, Executions Are Daily Occurrences at North Korea's 'Rehabilitation' Gulags." *National Post* (Toronto), February 3, 2012. http://news .nationalpost.com/2012/02/03/torture-executions-are-daily-occurrences-at-north -koreas-rehabilitation-gulags.

"Kazakhstan: No Accountability for Entrenched Torture." Amnesty International, July 11, 2013. http://www.amnesty.org/en/news/kazakhstan-no-accountability-entrenched -torture-2013-07-11.

Kelso, Paul. "Saudi Bomb Victim's Torture Ordeal—and Britain's Silence." *Guardian* (London), January 31, 2002. http://www.theguardian.com/world/2002/jan/31 /saudiarabia.politics.

Kiriakou, John. *The Reluctant Spy: My Secret Life in the CIA's War on Terror*. With Michael Ruby. New York: Bantam Books, 2009.

Kurczy, Stephen. "For Former Khmer Rouge Prisoners, Reparations Are Key to Justice." *Christian Science Monitor*, July 3, 2009.

Lindley, Robin. "Torture in Democratic Societies: Interview with Darius Rejali." *George Mason University's History News Network*. Accessed April 17, 2014. http://hnn.us/article /51419.

Matthias, Willard C. *America's Strategic Blunders: Intelligence Analysis and National Security Policy, 1936–1991*. University Park: Pennsylvania State University Press, 2001.

McCain, John. *Faith of My Fathers*. With Mark Salter. New York: Random House, 1999.

McKeon, Mark J. "Why We Must Prosecute." *Washington Post*, April 28, 2009. http://www.washingtonpost.com/wp-dyn/content/article/2009/04/27/AR2009042702693 .html.

O'Connor, Anne Marie, and William Booth. "Torture Surges in Mexico's Drug War, Rights Group Says." *Washington Post*, November 9, 2011. http://www.washingtonpost.com /world/americas/torture-surges-in-mexicos-drug-war-rights-group-says/2011/11/09 /gIQAphSI6M_story.html.

Ortiz, Dianna. "Dianna Ortiz." Robert F. Kennedy Center for Justice and Human Rights. 2014. Accessed April 17, 2014. http://rfkcenter.org/dianna-ortiz-7.

Pincus, Walter. "CIA Manual Discussed 'Coercive' Interrogation; Latin Countries Used 1983 Training Book." *Washington Post*, January 28, 1997.

Rejali, Darius. *Torture and Democracy*. Princeton, NJ: Princeton University Press, 2007.

Savage, Charlie. "Election to Decide Future Interrogation Methods in Terrorism Cases." *New York Times*, September 28, 2012.

Shue, Henry. "Torture." *In Torture: A Collection*, edited by Sanford Levinson, 47–60. Oxford: Oxford University Press, 2004.

Solzhenitsyn, Aleksandr I. *The Gulag Archipelago*. New York: Harper & Row, 1974.

Stanek, Steven. "Egyptian Bloggers Expose Horrors of Police Torture." *San Francisco Chronicle*, October 9, 2007. http://www.sfgate.com/politics/article/Egyptian-bloggers -expose-horror-of-police-torture-2536284.php.

"Terrorist Video Shows American Pleading." *CNN*, December 26, 2013. http:// transcripts.cnn.com/TRANSCRIPTS/1312/26/cnr.09.html.

"UAE: Reports of Systematic Torture in Jails." Human Rights Watch, June 27, 2013. http://www.hrw.org/news/2013/06/27/uae-reports-systematic-torture-jails.

What Went Wrong: Torture and the Office of Legal Counsel in the Bush Administration: Hearing Before the Subcommittee of Administrative Oversight and the Courts of the Committee on the Judiciary United States Senate. 111th Cong. (May 13, 2009) (Statement of Ali Soufan). http://www.judiciary.senate.gov/hearings/testimony.cfm?id=e655f9e2809 e5476862f735da14945e6&wit_id=e655f9e2809e5476862f735da14945e6-1-2.

Wisnewski, J. Jeremy. *Understanding Torture*. Edinburgh, UK: University Press, 2010.

FOR FURTHER INFORMATION

Books

Carlson, Julie A., and Elisabeth Weber, eds. *Speaking about Torture*. Bronx, NY: Fordham University Press, 2012.

Friedman, Lauri S., ed. *Human Rights*. Detroit: Greenhaven Press, 2010.

——. *Torture*. Detroit: Greenhaven Press, 2011.

Miller, Mara. *Remembering September 11, 2001: What We Know Now*. Berkeley Heights, NJ: Enslow, 2010.

Ortiz, Dianna (with Patricia Davis). *The Blindfold's Eyes: My Journey from Torture to Truth*. Maryknoll, New York: Orbis Books, 2002.

Perera, Anna. *Guantanamo Boy*. Park Ridge, IL: Albert Whitman & Company, 2011.

Rivera, Oscar Lopez. *Between Torture and Resistance*. Oakland, CA: PM Press, 2013.

Roleff, Tamara L., ed. *At Issue: Is Torture Ever Justified?* Detroit: Greenhaven Press, 2011.

Sterngass, Jon. *Terrorism*. New York: Marshall Cavendish, 2011.

Wein, Elizabeth. *Code Name Verity*. New York: Disney-Hyperion, 2013.

Websites

Amnesty International USA
> http://www.amnestyusa.org
> The Amnesty International website includes information on human rights abuses, including torture. By entering the word *torture* into the site's search engine, you can find reports on how torture is practiced in the twenty-first century.

Bernard Gui's *Conduct of Inquiry Concerning Heretical Depravity*
> http://www.fordham.edu/halsall/source/bernardgui-inq.asp
> Maintained by Fordham University in New York, the website contains an English translation of Bernard Gui's torture manual, *Conduct of Inquiry Concerning Heretical Depravity*. The document, written in the early 1300s, describes Gui's techniques for interrogating suspected heretics.

Center for Victims of Torture
> http://www.cvt.org
> Located in Saint Paul, Minnesota, the center provides counseling and other services to victims of torture. Visitors to the website can find information on the center's work on behalf of torture victims, including techniques used in the healing process and firsthand accounts from survivors.

Torture Museum
> http://www.torturemuseum.nl
> Located in Amsterdam in the Netherlands, the Torture Museum features a number of exhibits chronicling the history of torture. The museum's website provides information on the history of torture as well as images of torture devices used over the centuries.

The United States and the Geneva Conventions
  http://www.cfr.org/international-law/united-states-geneva-conventions
  /p11485
  Maintained by the Council on Foreign Relations, the website provides background
  on the Geneva Conventions and how the United States approached the Geneva
  Conventions following the 2001 terrorist attacks to justify its practice of enhanced
  interrogation.

Waterboarding: A Tortured History
  http://www.npr.org/2007/11/03/15886834/waterboarding-a-tortured
  -history
  This site is a companion to a 2007 National Public Radio report on the history of
  waterboarding. The site examines the debate over the waterboarding of terrorism
  suspects, plus images and information about waterboarding over the centuries.

FILMS

Taxi to the Dark Side
  DVD, Discovery Channel, 2007
  The 2007 film, directed by Alex Gibney, won an Academy Award for Best
  Documentary Feature. It chronicles the enhanced interrogation techniques
  employed by military officers at the prison on the grounds of the US airfield in
  Bagram, Afghanistan.

The Torture Question
  http://www.pbs.org/wgbh/pages/frontline/torture/
  Public Broadcasting Service, 2005
  Part of the PBS *Frontline* series, this show traces the history of how decisions made
  in Washington, DC, after 9/11 laid the groundwork for prisoner abuse in Iraq;
  Afghanistan; and Guantanamo Bay, Cuba.

Zero Dark Thirty
  DVD, Columbia Pictures, 2012
  This film, directed by Kathryn Bigelow, presents a fictionalized account of the
  decadelong hunt for al-Qaeda leader Osama bin Laden in the years after the
  September 11, 2001, terrorist attacks and his killing by US Army Special Forces in
  2011. The movie includes some vivid scenes of torture.

LERNER

SOURCE™

Expand learning beyond the printed book. Download free, complementary
educational resources for this book from our website, www.lerneresource.com.

INDEX

Gui, Bernard, 16–17, 96

hazing, 87
heresy, 16
homosexuality, 20, 30, 83
human rights organizations, 6–7, 69, 79.
    See also activists and advocacy groups
Human Rights Watch (HRW), 30, 35, 82
Hussein, Saddam, 30, 70, 92

instruments of torture, 27–29, 77
International Committee of the Red Cross,
    44
International Criminal Court (ICC), 76, 98
International Olympic Committee (IOC),
    84
International Rehabilitation Council for
    Torture Victims, 69
interrogations: without torture, 32, 60–61;
    with torture, 7, 16, 25, 38, 51, 55, 57–59,
    64, 71, 76–77, 87–90
Iraq War, 36, 70, 86. *See also* War on
    Terror

journalists, 30, 54, 56, 63, 80

Khmer Rouge, 66, 78–79, 98–99

McCain, John, 64
medical experiments, 20–21, 97
Mengele, Josef, 20
Middle Ages, 13–17
Middle East, 80–82
Milosevic, Slobodan, 75–77, 98
modern torture: in Africa, 28–29; and cell
    phones, 80, 82; in China, 84, 99; and
    the Internet, 80–81; in Latin America,
    54–57; in the Middle East, 30–31,
    39–40; and television, 31–33; in the
    United States, 36–39
Mohammed, Khalid Sheikh, 58, 62, 99
Moore, Peter, 70–71
Mubarak, Hosni, 80–82

National Intelligence Directorate, 54

Nazis, 19–22, 32, 97. *See also* concentration
    camps; Gestapo; medical experiments
9/11, 57–59, 92
North Atlantic Treaty Organization
    (NATO), 75–76
Northup, Solomon, 18–19

Obama, Barack, 64, 76
Ortiz, Dianna, 55–56

Pearl Harbor, 52
Physicians for Human Rights, 74–75
post-traumatic stress disorder (PTSD),
    67–68
prisoners of war, 17, 49, 92
prisons, 15, 19, 22–25, 27, 36, 55, 58,
    66, 79. *See also* Abu Ghraib prison;
    concentration camps; Soviet Gulag
prosecutions and convictions, 22, 38, 75
psychological torture, 33, 35

Qaeda, al-, 31–33, 61, 87–88, 92, 98

Roosevelt, Eleanor, 48

School of the Americas (SOA), 50–57, 72,
    98
secret police forces, 21, 22–23, 28, 54. *See
    also* Gestapo
Shumba, Gabriel, 85–86
slavery, 17–19, 44, 97. *See also* Northrup,
    Solomon
Solzhenitsyn, Aleksandr I., 23–24
Soviet Gulag, 22–24, 97
Spartacus, 11, 96
Stalin, Joseph, 22–23

terrorism, 57–59
torture: in ancient times, 7, 9–12;
    and monetary compensation,
    77–79; arguments against, 41–42, 63;
    arguments for, 62; of children, 21,
    27–28, 55, 81–82; in Colonial America,
    17–19; during the Enlightenment,
    41–43; and government approval of,

PHOTO ACKNOWLEDGMENTS

The images in this book are used with the permission of: Backgrounds: © iStockphoto.com/
flyfloor (scratched background); © iStockphoto.com/loops7 (concrete wall); © iStockphoto.com/
cla78 (frames); © Dragoneye/Dreamstime.com, p. 1; Courtesy of Front Line Defenders, p. 4; © Old
Time/Alamy, p. 6; © Gualtiero Boffi/Dreamstime.com, p. 8; © Iberfoto/SuperStock, p. 10; © The
Damned Field, Execution place in the Roman Empire, 1878 (oil on canvas), Bronnikov, Fedor
Andreevich (1827–1902/Tretyakov Gallery, Moscow, Russia/Bridgeman Images, p. 12; Wikimedia
Commons (public domain), p. 14; © Leemage/UIG via Getty Images, p. 16; © Time Life Pictures/
War Department/National Archives/Time Life Pictures/Getty Images, p. 18; Sovfoto Universal
Images Group/Newscom, p. 22; © AFP/Getty Images, p. 26, AP Photo/Ng Han Guan, p. 28; AP
Photo/Erasing 76 Crimes, p. 30; Courtesy Wikipedia/ZUMA Press/Newscom, p. 37, © The Gallery
Collection/CORBIS, p. 43; © MPI/Getty Images, p. 45; Kevin T. Quinn/Wikimedia Commons
(Attribution 2.0 Generic) , p. 47; © Fotosearch/Getty Images, p. 48; © Tom Williams/Roll Call/
Getty Images, p. 50; © Universal History Archive/Getty Images, p. 53; © Jim West/Alamy, p. 56;
© Spencer Plat/Getty Images, p. 58; © Peter Muhly/AFP/Getty Images, p. 65; © John Bryson//Time
Life Pictures/Getty Images, p. 66; Nancee E. Lewis/U-T San Diego/ZUMAPRESS/Newscom, p. 68; The
Washington Times/ZUMAPRESS/Newscom, p. 72; © Mosa'ab Elshamy/FlickrVision/Getty Images,
p. 81; AP Photo/Ben Curtis, p. 83; © Peter Kramer/NBC/NBC NewsWire via Getty Image, p. 88; AP
Photo/Mary Altaffer, p. 89.

Front Cover: © iStockphoto.com/spxChrome, (thumbscrew); © iStockphoto.com/flyfloor (scratched
background); © iStockphoto.com/loops7 (concrete wall).

ABOUT THE AUTHOR

Hal Marcovitz is a former newspaper reporter and columnist. He has written more than 170 books for young readers. He makes his home in Bucks County, Pennsylvania.